Duncan J. D. Smith

ONLY IN
SEVILLE

A Guide to Unique Locations,
Hidden Corners and Unusual Objects

Photographs by
Duncan J. D. Smith
except where stated otherwise

**The
Urban
Explorer**

The Baths of Doña Maria de Padilla beneath the Real Alcázar (see no. 1)

Contents

Introduction

"Like Spain, I'm bound to the past."
William S. Burroughs, *Cities of the Red Night*, 1981

This terse observation well reflects Seville since much of the Andalucian capital is a palimpsest. Consider Seville Cathedral, with its Moorish minaret and Visigothic font, or the Alameda de Hércules, a plaza where street cafés join Roman columns on a former riverbed. These places imbue the city with a haunting sense of history, one that intrigues locals and visitors alike.

Seville occupies a plain on a bend in the Guadalquivir River, Spain's only great navigable waterway. With access to the Atlantic at Cádiz and a backdrop of mineral-rich mountains, the city was long coveted as a staging post by a colourful roster of invaders. All have left their mark.

The Phoenicians came first in the 8th century BC (although a sophisticated Iberian culture already existed). Trading ceramics for precious metals, they founded Hisbaal in honour of their god Baal. Later, in 206 BC, the Romans appeared during a war with the Carthaginians. Attracted by the wealth of the Iberian Peninsula, they divided it into provinces. Hisbaal found itself in Baetica and became the trading colony of Hispalis, exporting olive oil and wheat to Rome.

Baetica's success was prolonged by the Visigoths, a Germanic tribe, who arrived from northern Europe in 415 AD. They remained until 711, when Umayyad Muslims based in Syria made the peninsula part of their caliphate. Baetica was renamed al-Andalus and Hispalis became Ishbiliyya (hence eventually Seville). Moorish Andalucia, named by Europeans after Mauretania, the Roman name for North Africa, was defined by its mosques, orange trees and a love of poetry.

The fragmentation of the caliphate in the 11th century made way for the Abbadids, Almoravids and eventually the Almohads from Morocco, who made Seville their European capital. They held sway until 1248, when King Ferdinand III of Castile (1201–1252) captured the city as part of the Reconquest of the Iberian Peninsula. Following Columbus's establishment in 1492 of the first permanent European settlement in the Americas, Andalucia entered a Golden Age, with Seville flourishing as Europe's gateway to the New World. The vast wealth this generated during the 16th and early 17th centuries facilitated the construction of palaces and churches making Seville a symbol of Spanish imperial might.

By the 1680s the Guadalquivir had silted up and Seville's role as a port declined. Habsburgs and Bourbons occupied the Spanish throne and a series of wars and plagues reduced Andalucia to one of Spain's poorest regions. In spite of this both *flamenco* and *tapas* originated in the region during the 18th and 19th centuries.

Civil strife tainted the first half of the 20th century and the region's revival only really took off following the death of Franco in 1975. In 1982, Andalucia became an autonomous community *(comunidad autónom)* and a few years later Spain acceded to the European Union. Subsequent investment has seen Seville evolve rapidly into a modern city, with a healthy tourist sector trading on its mercurial past.

Only in Seville is designed for city explorers interested in getting under the city's skin. This is the Seville of grand palaces and closed convents, artistic havens and secluded patios, fervent traditions and epicurean delights. The fifty-five locations described represent the author's odyssey in and around the city's five central areas (a combination of official districts and neighbourhoods known as *barrios*), which together showcase Seville's treasures old and new.

The first, Santa Cruz, lies at the heart of the formerly walled Old Town *(Casco Antiguo)*. Muslim Seville was here and later the *Judería* or Jewish Quarter. The neighbourhood's warren of narrow streets holds many key sites, including the Gothic Seville Cathedral, with its landmark Giralda, and the Real Alcázar palace.

As its name suggests, the neighbourhood of El Arenal was originally a sandy area on the banks of the Guadalquivir. Once the port of Seville – the medieval shipyards are still extant – it is now built up and home to the city's bullring.

To the north is La Macarena. A traditional district dotted with churches and convents, its namesake basilica is the focus of Seville's annual Holy Week (Semana Santa). The bustling Calle de la Feria provides a glimpse of everyday life in the city.

Across the river is working class Triana, which boasts a centuries-old association with ceramic manufacturing and is the spiritual home to *flamenco*. It is flanked by the Isla de la Cartuja, which hosted Seville's Expo '92, and Los Remedios, home to the famous Seville April Fair.

Back across the river and south of Santa Cruz is leafy Parque de María Luisa. Once private gardens alongside Seville's Royal Tobacco Factory, it was remodelled for the Ibero–American Exposition of 1929. The former pavilions now serve a variety of cultural purposes.

Although Seville is Spain's fourth largest city and well served by buses and trams, walking is the best way to get around. Whether marvelling at the water cistern beneath the Real Alcázar, sipping sherry in the oldest *tapas* bar, crossing Santiago Calatrava's suspension bridge, or scaling the world's largest wooden structure, *Only in Seville* will encourage readers to set out on their own urban expedition.

1 Europe's Oldest Royal Palace

Santa Cruz, the Real Alcázar de Sevilla on Plaza del Triunfo (note: book tickets in advance to avoid queues www.alcazarsevilla.org)

The Real Alcázar de Sevilla is Europe's oldest royal palace still in use. First built as a fortified palace by the Moors, it was converted after the Reconquest by Spain's Catholic monarchs into a royal residence. With buildings and gardens spanning a thousand years, it is little wonder UNESCO has listed it among their World Heritage Sites.

Despite its singular name, the Real Alcázar comprises a dozen palaces built at different times and in different styles. These have survived to varying degrees having undergone remodelling and in some cases demolition. A well-considered tour takes in remains that are Moorish, Gothic, *Mudéjar* and Renaissance, with gardens to match.

All tours begin at the Puerta del León (Lion Gate), which opens off the Plaza del Triunfo (Santa Cruz). The distinctive crenellated walls here that once encircled Seville's Old Town (Casco Antiguo) represent the visitor's first brush with things Moorish. They were commissioned in 1023 by Abad I (984–1042), founder of the Abbadid dynasty and first independent Muslim ruler of Seville, as protection against Christian forces (see no. 37).

The word *alcázar* comes from the Arabic *al-qasr* meaning 'the fort, castle or palace'. The first was built on the site of a Visigothic basilica in 913 by Abd al-Rahman III (891–961), caliph of the

Mudéjar architecture at the Real Alcázar de Sevilla

Umayyads. It was the fragmentation of the Umayyad caliphate during the 11th century that made way for the Abbadids, including the poet-king Al-Mu'tamid (1040–1094), who enlarged the Alcázar creating the so-called Al Mubarak Palace. Subsequently the Almohads made Seville their European capital and built their own Alcázar. To see a precious fragment of this structure, the earliest still standing, enter the Patio del León (Courtyard of the Lion) and turn left into the Hall of Justice (Sala de la Justicia). Here, in the Patio del Yeso (Courtyard of Plaster), is a portico made from Moorish perforated stone screens *(tsebka)* on slender columns, backed by a double-horsehoe arch.

Now return to the Patio del León and pass through a weathered masonry arch to reach the Patio de la Montería (the Al Mubarak Palace once stood here). The arcaded wing on the right was commissioned by Queen Isabella I of Castile (1451–1504) and is clearly European in style. It was here in the Casa de la Contratación (Contracting House) that navigators were despatched to explore and exploit the New World on behalf of Spain. This is where Columbus planned his second voyage and Magellan sought support for his circumnavigation. A chapel dedicated to the Virgin of the Navigators (La Virgen de los Navegantes) contains an altarpiece depicting the blond-haired Columbus and a group of what he termed 'Indians' protected under the Virgin Mary's mantle. This wing today is used by the reigning Spanish monarch when in Seville.

Back in the Patio de la Montería, and on the right is the Palacio Pedro I. Undoubtedly the most recognised incarnation of the Alcázar, this magnificent example of *Mudéjar* (Christian Moorish) architecture, designed and built by Muslim artisans retained after the Reconquest, was commissioned by King Peter I of Castile (1334–1369) (see no. 15). It has three main elements. First is the elegant Patio de las Doncellas (Court of the Maidens), with its *Mudéjar* polylobed arcade supporting a Renaissance balcony. Reserved for ceremonies and entertaining, it features a reflecting pool flanked by orange trees, sunken so that their blossoms and fruit could be fully appreciated. Second is the more intimate Patio de las Muñecas (Court of the Dolls) around which are ranged the palace's domestic quarters. Again in *Mudéjar* style, the intricate plasterwork includes not only Koranic inscriptions but also figures of animals and kings prohibited under Islam (the name refers to two tiny heads carved onto one of the arches.). The third element is the Salón de Embajaries (Ambassadors' Hall) added in 1427. Its triple-horseshoe arches are surrounded by plasterwork and geometric tiles *(azulejos)* topped off with a stunning *media naranja* (half orange) dome made from carved and gilded wood.

Beneath the palace is a secret. A tunnel in the walled back garden leads to the Baths of Doña Maria de Padilla (see frontispiece). Erroneously named for the king's wife, these atmospheric vaulted chambers are actually rainwater cisterns for the gardens. Like the palace, the gardens themselves reflect different styles – from intricate Moorish gardens nearest the palace to the less contrived gardens of the Spanish kings beyond (watch out for the rare 17th century hydraulic organ). They are especially romantic when visited as part of a night-time guided tour.

Evidence for further phases of palace construction can be found

Glorious gardens at the Real Alcázar

by re-entering the Alcázar behind the Estanque de Mercurio (Pond of Mercury), with its impressive terracotta water spout. Here the 13th century Gothic palace of King Alfonso X (1221–1284) was reworked in the 16th century as a Renaissance palace for Holy Roman Emperor Charles V (1500–1558). Its impressive Gothic Vault Hall is lined with figurative painted tiles and Renaissance tapestries. It was Charles' marriage to Isabella of Portugal (1503–1539) that forged a powerful union of two great royal houses.

The Alcázar has proven a popular filming location. In *The Wind and the Lion* (1975) it doubles as a Sultan's palace in Fez. In *Kingdom of Heaven* (2005) it served as the court of the King of Jerusalem, and more recently in the television series *Game of Thrones* it has been the Water Gardens of Dorne.

Other locations nearby: 2, 3, 4, 5, 6, 13

2   A Superlative Cathedral

**Santa Cruz, Seville Cathedral (Catedral de Sevilla) on Avenida
de la Constitución (note: book tickets in advance to avoid queues
www.catedraldesevilla.es)**

Seville's architectural superlative is its cathedral. The world's largest
Gothic building (and the third largest church in Europe), its cavern-
ous interior could swallow an upended football pitch. No wonder the
Reconquista Christians who built it bragged "We'll build a cathedral so
huge that anyone who sees us will take us for mad men"!

Before entering the Cathedral of Saint Mary of the See (Catedral de
Santa María de la Sede), as the building is known officially, consider
its exterior. Dominating the east façade is the Giralda, once the minaret of Seville's Almohad-era mosque. Completed in 1198, it contains a
spiral ramp illuminated by double polylobed windows *(ajimez)*, each
set in a decorative brick frame *(alfiz)* flanked by brickwork panels of
arabesques *(tsebka)*. It is the city's foremost Moorish survival.

The Christians retained the mosque for use as a church until 1356,
when an earthquake caused it serious damage. This prompted the
erection of a new building, the construction of which spanned several
centuries though the style remained predominantly Gothic. The minaret survived thanks to its sturdy foundation of reused Roman masonry
but it lost its crowning gilded spheres. Instead in 1568 a Renaissance-
style belfry was added, capped by a female figural weathervane representing Christianity triumphant. The whole is known today as La
Giralda meaning 'she who turns'.

The north façade of the cathedral is obscured by later structures,
including the Iglesia del Sagrario parish church and the Biblioteca
Columbina. The central doorway, however, the Puerta del Perdón
(Door of Pardon), with its *kufic*-smothered bronze panels, is another
remnant of the Almohad mosque, which originally gave access to the
mosque's ablutions' yard (see no. 3). Note, too, the red-painted *graffiti*
– so-called *Victores* ('hurrahs') – added by 16th century students celebrating the completion of their doctorates.

The west façade is the Gothic cathedral in all its pinnacled and
buttressed glory. Note the sculptural detail of the doorways and the
superb rose window. The chained columns in front were probably salvaged from the Roman city of Itálica.

The south façade is again obscured by later building so it's best
to step back and admire instead the Gothic roofline, which can be

experienced up-close on a rooftop tour. The main entrance, the Puerta del Principe (Door of the Prince), is located here. The cathedral's interior occupies the rectangular footprint of the former mosque – roughly 400 by 600 feet – and comprises five east–west naves separated by columns supporting the vaulted roof. The outermost columns frame a series of side chapels with wrought iron screens *(rejas)* and Flemish stained-glass windows. The central nave is the widest and highest. It contains an enclosed choir for more intimate services, as well as the Capilla Mayor (Main Chapel), with its towering gilded altarpiece. Carved in the 1480s and depicting the life of Christ

La Giralda seen from behind the walls of the Real Alcázar

in forty scenes, it is 120 feet high. Behind this is the Capilla Real (Royal Chapel), a Renaissance-era addition with a cupola and hemispherical apse smothered in *plateresque* stucco. Here the faithful worship a statue of the Virgen de los Reyes (Virgin of the Kings), patron saint of Seville, at whose feet rests the body of King Ferdinand III of Castile (1201–1252) in a silver sarcophagus.

The southern transept contains the remains of explorer Christopher Columbus (1451–1506), his coffin held aloft by four pall-bearers representing the medieval kingdoms that became Spain (Aragon, Castille, León and Navarre). Adjacent is the Sacristia Mayor (Main Sacristy), which contains paintings by Bartolomé Esteban Murillo (1617–1682) and a reliquary made for King Alfonso X of Castile (1221–1284) containing fragments of saintly tooth and bone.

Other locations nearby: 1, 3, 4, 5, 22, 23

3 The Courtyard of the Orange Trees

Santa Cruz, the Patio de los Naranjos (Courtyard of the Orange Trees) at Seville Cathedral (Catedral de Sevilla) on Avenida de la Constitución (note: book tickets in advance to avoid queues www.catedraldesevilla.es)

In 1492, during his first voyage to the Americas, Christopher Columbus (1451–1506) described the air as being "soft as that of Seville in April, and so fragrant that it was delicious to breathe it". Seville's distinct perfume came from its orange trees, which still impress today with their colour and number. Approximately 50,000 of them adorn busy streets and secluded courtyards alike. There are two times in the year when they are at their best. The first is between December and February, when the fruits are ripe. The second is late March, when for about three weeks the city is cloaked in white blossom generating the scent that so beguiled Columbus.

A good place to reflect on this urban phenomenon is the Patio de los Naranjos (Courtyard of the Orange Trees) at Seville Cathedral (Catedral de Sevilla) (Santa Cruz) (see no. 2). The footprint of the courtyard corresponds with that of the ablutions' yard of the Almohad mosque that once stood here. The Moorish fountain in the centre is fashioned from a Visigothic font, one of the few tangible remains from the city's immediate post-Roman history. The orange trees planted a century ago are Seville's oldest although according to Spanish historian Rodrigo Caro (1573–1647) oranges have been growing here since at least the 16th century. Perhaps they provided shade for the Almohads, too.

It is the bitter orange *(Citrus aurantium)* that grows in Seville. Originating in Southeast Asia, it appeared first in the wild as a cross between mandarin and pomelo parents. It was introduced into the Eastern Roman Empire from India around the 1st century and then spread gradually throughout the eastern Mediterranean and North Africa. It found its way to Andalucia courtesy of the Moors as early as the 8th century, as did the name. The Sanskrit word for orange is *naranga* (meaning 'inner fragrance') from which came the Arabic *naranj*, Spanish *naranja* and eventually the English *orange*.

The Moors didn't grow bitter oranges for eating though. Rather they appreciated the shade provided by their lush evergreen leaves. They also pioneered complex irrigation techniques to support orange orchards, the blossoms from which were harvested for use in perfumes and healing oils. By the time the Spanish reconquered Andalucia, orange trees were being planted in public spaces. Bitter oranges were a good choice because the trees remained attractive all year round and the fruits were ignored by peckish passers-by!

Only in the 17th century, when sugar from Caribbean plantations became readily available, were large-scale culinary uses found for bitter oranges. Notably during the 18th century a Scotsman speculatively bought a cargo of Seville oranges and used the pectin-rich fruit to make Seville Orange Marmalade.

Orange trees bring colour and shade to the streets of Seville

Since then a significant quantity of oranges has been exported to Britain for the same purpose. Those that remain are used by local convents to make their house marmalades and sweets – *mermelada* and *yemas* respectively – or else they are left to rot on the ground (see no. 34). More recently, however, Seville's water utility company Emasesa has piloted a scheme whereby the juice of unwanted fruit is used to generate gas rich in methane, which in turn is used to create clean energy for one of its purification plants. The remaining skin and seeds are used as organic fertiliser.

The Moorish Puerta del Lagarto (Gate of the Lizard) in one corner of the Patio de los Naranjos is named for the suspended crocodile said to have been a gift from an Egyptian emir seeking the hand of a Spanish *infanta*.

Other locations nearby: 2, 5, 20, 22, 23

4   The Archive of the Indies

Santa Cruz, the General Archive of the Indies (Archivo General
de Indias) on Avenida de la Constitución (note: contents of the
archive can be viewed by appointment only)

The Jardines de Murillo were once orchards of the Real Alcázar.
Donated to the city in 1911, they are named for the renowned Golden
Age artist Bartolomé Esteban Murillo (1617–1682) (see no. 28). In
among the monumental fig trees is a twin-columned monument to
Christopher Columbus (1451–1506). It incorporates a model of the
Santa María, the caravel that famously bore him in 1492 from Spain
to the New World.

Between 1503 and 1680, Spain had a monopoly on the lucrative
and exploitative trade that ultimately resulted from Columbus' travels.
With treasure fleets returning regularly from the Americas – or the
Indies as they were known – a colonial administration was created
to orchestrate trade on both sides of the Atlantic. This resulted in a
vast amount of documentation, which was initially stored in archives
in Seville, Cádiz and Simancas. Lack of space, however, in the main
archive in Simancas meant that in 1785 by decree of King Charles III
(1716–1788) the archives were merged in Seville as the General Archive of the Indies (Archivo General de Indias).

Located on Avenida de la Constitución (Santa Cruz), the building
housing the General Archive was originally designed with a different
purpose in mind. It was commissioned in 1572 by King Philip II (1527–
1598) as a merchants' exchange (Casa Lonja de Mercaderes), where
valuable commodities from the Americas were traded (until that point
Seville's merchants had conducted their business in the cool recesses
of the cathedral). The architect was Juan de Herrera (1530–1597), a
man renowned for his work on the Escorial palace outside Madrid. His
sobre, unfussy Herreran Style deployed in both buildings represents
the zenith of Renaissance architecture in Spain. In Seville, it is manifested in the two-storey façades, which are unadorned except for the
roof balustrade and obelisks, the building's appeal lying instead in the
discreet contrasting tonalities of stone and stucco, and the shadows
cast by the modest pilasters and window surrounds.

As an archive, the former exchange lent itself perfectly, with its
long corridors and tall, arched windows overlooking a large internal
patio. Most importantly the building was available, since by 1785 most
of Seville's commerce had passed to Cádiz. The first cartloads of docu-

A book on piracy at the General Archive of the Indies

ments arrived later the same year and a grand marble staircase was installed to enable visitors to access them easily.

Today the General Archive boasts an impressive 43,000 volumes on five and a half miles of shelving representing the written and printed output of the various offices of Spain's colonial administration. Chief among them was the Seville-based Casa de la Contratación de las Indias (House of Trade of the Indies), which from 1503 onwards administered everything from commissioning maps to assessing probate of estates of Spaniards dying overseas.

These days the archive's 80 million pages are in the process of being digitised for online access although nothing beats the experience of seeing the material *in situ* (by appointment only). Pride of place goes to Columbus' annotated copy of the *Almanach Perpetuum* by Abraham Zacuto (1452–c.1515), which enabled him to calculate latitude correctly. There is also the Papal Bull *Inter Caetera* of 1493 supporting Spain's exclusive claim to lands discovered by Columbus. Other items include books on piracy, plans of colonial American cities and Miguel de Cervantes' unsuccessful request for a posting overseas.

Much of the gold and silver brought from the Indies was stored in the Royal Mint of Seville (Real Casa de la Moneda de Sevilla). Completed in 1598, and operational until the 19th century, it stands close to the General Archive, on Calle Santander.

Other locations nearby: 1, 2, 3, 5, 22, 23

5 The Virgin's Square

Santa Cruz, a stroll around the Plaza Virgen de los Reyes

The Plaza Virgen de los Reyes bustles with people making their way to Seville Cathedral, the world's largest Gothic structure, where an effigy of the 'Virgin of the Kings' is venerated (see no. 2). Those in less of a rush, however, should pause outside and contemplate the plaza itself, which is a veritable *tableau vivant* of Sevillian motifs: stately buildings, orange trees and horsedrawn carriages, all set against an azure blue sky. This is Seville as imagined by many visitors.

Despite being overshadowed by the cathedral, the buildings surrounding the plaza warrant a closer look. Consider, for example, the red-and-white Archbishop's Palace (Palacio Arzobispal) on the northern side. It was begun in the mid-16th century hence its overall Renaissance appearance. That it was not completed until the 18th century, however, is demonstrated by the ornate Sevillian Baroque portal bolted onto the façade giving access to two internal courtyards. One of these once housed an archbishop's pet lion!

Inside, the palace has a magnificent coloured marble staircase, a frescoed ceiling by Antonio Mohedano (1561–1625), and paintings by the Golden Age artists Bartolomé Esteban Murillo (1617–1682), Francisco de Zurbarán (1598–1664) and Francisco Herrera (1576–1656). Clearly impressed by such grandeur, Marshall-General Soult (1769–1851), Napoleon's military commander during the French occupation of Seville in 1810, commandeered the place. These days it is back in the hands of the clergy.

In front of the palace stands a fine lantern-topped fountain by José Lafita Diáz (1887–1945), son of the acclaimed landscape artist José Lafita y Blanco (1852–1925). It was installed to impress visitors to Seville during the city's Ibero–American Exposition of 1929 (Exposición iberoamericana de 1929) (see no. 20).

The southern side of the plaza is occupied by the Convento de la Encarnación, which was founded in 1404 following the destruction of the nearby Jewish Quarter. With its whitewashed walls and triple-pierced belfry, it has a Mediterranean feel that provides a satisfying counterpoint to the Renaissance palace and the cathedral's bare Gothic stone. A plaque hereabouts recalls that until the 18th century, the plaza was the Corral de los Olmos (Courtyard of the Elms), a cluster of Church buildings referred to in the writings of Cervantes. Earlier still the Moors had their first mosque here, and before that the Romans had

The Plaza Virgen de los Reyes is Seville as imagined by visitors

a bath building, the remains of which lie beneath the Archbishop's Palace.

The plaza narrows as it squeezes between the cathedral and convent, and as it does it changes name. The Plaza del Triunfo commemorates Seville's survival following the Great Lisbon Earthquake of 1755, the tsunami from which swept right up the Guadalquivir River. Salvation was attributed to Seville's fervent devotion to the Virgin Mary, who is honoured by a Baroque column, as well as a modern monument. The Immaculate Conception (La Inmaculada Concepción) is celebrated here each December 8th by wandering minstrels.

This plaza is also overlooked by the cathedral, as well as by the imposing Archive of the Indies (Archivo General de Indias) and the crenellated walls of the Real Alcázar (see nos. 1, 4). It is worth noting, too, that Seville's City Hall (Ayuntamiento) was once located here before its relocation to the Plaza de San Francisco (see no. 19).

A special time to visit the Plaza Virgen de los Reyes is during Easter Holy Week (Semana Santa) since it is located on the official procession route. It is a great place to watch the hooded *nazarenos* of the city's church brotherhoods (*cofradias*) passing solemnly by (see no. 38).

Other locations nearby: 1, 2, 3, 4, 6

6 Old Priests, Old Masters

Santa Cruz, the Hospital de los Venerables Sacerdotes at 8 Plaza Venerables

In the early 1990s, one of Seville's fine Baroque buildings saw a radical change of function. For over three centuries the Hospital de los Venerables Sacerdotes had served as a comfortable residence for elderly priests. When the last of them departed during the 1970s, the building became home to a cultural foundation and art gallery. Old priests had been swapped for Old Masters!

The story of the Hospital goes back to 1627, when Seville's Brotherhood of Silence (Hermandad del Silencio) decided to assist the city's elderly and often impoverished priests. A rented house was used until 1675, when Justino de Neve (1625–1685), an influential canon of Seville Cathedral (Catedral de Sevilla), founded the purpose-built Hospital, which was completed in 1697 to designs by the renowned architect Leonardo de Figueroa (1654–1730).

Until 1805 the Hospital was funded by the Brotherhood, as well as by charity donations and the monarchy. Thereafter, wars and the loss of Spain's colonies saw funding decreased. Faced with bankruptcy, in 1840 the Brotherhood sold the Hospital to a textile manufacturer and the priests were relocated to Seville's Charity Hospital (Hospital de la Caridad) (see no. 23). Fortunately, in 1848 the priests were returned to their original home by royal decree, where they remained for the next 130 years.

At the heart of the Baroque building seen today is a large monastic-style cloister *(Claustro Mayor)* consisting of a central sunken fountain surrounded on four sides by Tuscan arcades. To one side is the former infirmary, once home to the priests, which consists of an arched rectangular hall (not usually accessible).

Flanking another side is a magnificent church completed in 1689 and dedicated to Saint Peter. The cupola and barrel-vaulted nave are covered in frescoes – many on the topic of priesthood – by the Baroque painter Juan de Valdés Leal (1622–1690) and his equally-talented son, Lucas de Valdés Carasquilla (1661–1725). The latter was responsible for *The Apotheosis of St. Ferdinand*, which can be seen top centre in the main altarpiece *(retablo mayor)*. Notice, too, the altar frieze inscribed in Greek ("Fear God and Honour the Priest") and the side chapels containing priestly relics, and a pulpit fashioned from exotic woods.

The main courtyard of the Hospital de los Venerables Sacerdotes

Off the third side of the *patio* is a vaulted staircase adorned with a magnificent Baroque plaster heaven supported by cherubs. This leads to an upstairs cloister off which there are further rooms, including a library and a discreet balcony overlooking the church, which was used by priests too sick to attend Mass.

Since 1991, the Hospital has been home to the Focus Foundation (Fundación Focus), which does much to promote the cultural heritage of Seville. After restoring the Hospital, in 2007 it inaugurated the Velázquez Centre (Centro Velázquez) dedicated to the memory of the famous Seville-born painter. One of the Hospital's ground floor rooms has been adapted as a gallery space in which a small but valuable collection of paintings from the Spanish Golden Age are displayed. Pride of place goes to an intriguing portrait by Diego Velázquez (1599–1660) of *Santa Rufina* holding a feather and a tea cup (Rufina and her sister Justa are venerated in Seville for having been executed by the Roman authorities in the name of Christianity). Other works are by the likes of Francisco Pacheco (1564–1644), Francisco Varela (1580–1645), Francisco de Zurbarán (1598–1664) and Bartolomé Esteban Murillo (1617–1682), all of whom spent time in Seville.

Other locations nearby: 1, 5, 7, 10

7 Beneath Rosina's Balcony

Santa Cruz, a walk passing beneath Rosina's Balcony in Plaza Alfaro

The *barrio* Santa Cruz is Seville at its most romantic and condensed. Formerly encompassing the city's Jewish Quarter *(Judería)*, this maze of whitewashed alleys fell into disrepair when the Jews were expelled (see no. 10). After reinvention as a neighbourhood of well-to-do Christian homes, it again fell from grace only to be reborn in the early-20th century as a picturesque magnet for visitors.

This walk begins in the peaceful Plaza de Santa Cruz, with its intricate wrought iron well head (if the door is open, don't miss the traditional domestic *patio* at number 9). From here walk along Calle de Nicolás Antoni and turn right to reach Plaza Alfaro, where Seville's loveliest balcony overlooks the Jardines de Murillo. In a city famous for having inspired many operas, it is not difficult to imagine Count Almaviva in Rossini's *Il barbiere di Siviglia* scaling the wall here in pursuit of the lovely Rosina. Accordingly, the spot has long been known as Rosina's Balcony, its theatrical quality enhanced by an old fashioned lantern, orange tree and red geraniums.

Now walk west along Callejón del Agua, so called for the terracotta water pipes that can still be seen in the Alcázar's garden wall here. Of the old houses whose gardens front the alley, number 2 is where American author Washington Irving (1783–1859) lodged while conducting research in the city (see no. 8).

Next turn right onto Calle Pimienta, then left onto Calle Susona. This winds its way into the Plaza de Doña Elvira. In one corner is the house museum of Granada artist Amalio García del Moral y Garrido (1922–1995), who purchased the property for its view of the Giralda (see no. 11).

Leave the plaza by means of Calle Vida and turn right into the well-hidden Calle Judería. One of the Seville's old gates is here, the Postigo del Alcázar, beneath which pedestrians pass directly. This gives onto the Patio de Banderas, a large public square within the walls of the palace, where coronation ceremonies were staged. An archway at the far end opens out onto the Plaza del Triunfo in front of the cathedral (see no. 5).

Now turn right along Calle Joaquín Romero Murube to reach Plaza de la Alianza. Presided over by another of the Alcázar's towers, it contains a fountain and a tiled depiction of the Crucifixion. John Fulton

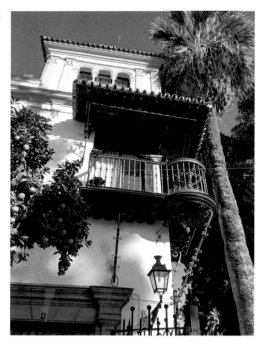

Rosina's Balcony overlooking the Jardines de Murillo

(1933–1998), the first American matador, had a home here and acted as a guide for novelist John Michener (1907–1997) when he visited to research his book *Iberia*.

Turn right down Calle de Rodrigo Caro to regain the Plaza de Doña Elvira. Now turn left in the far corner along Calle Gloria to reach the Plaza Venerables, then left again onto Calle Jamerdana and right onto Calle Reinosa. This is one of Seville's narrowest streets hence its nickname 'Callejón de los Besos' (Alley of the Kisses) because the balconies here almost touch each other. Such narrow streets help maximise shade during Seville's hot summers. At the end of Calle Reinosa turn right onto Calle Lope de Rueda, which runs all the way back to Plaza Alfaro.

Seville's balconies, whether rudimentary or more elegant in the form of glass and wrought iron loggias (*miradores*), are often a source of civic pride. Decorated with pot plants and flags all year round, a special effort is made on the occasion of Corpus Christi, when religious statues, woven palm fronds and even floral shawls (*mantoncillos*) are displayed.

Other locations nearby: 6, 8, 9, 10, 13

8 The Legend of Don Juan

Santa Cruz, the statue of Don Juan in the Plaza de Los Refinadores

With its mercurial history and penchant for hedonism, Seville has long attracted writers. From homegrown wordsmiths to curious visitors, each has been inspired by the city to create a distinct literary landscape. It makes for an interesting thematic tour to follow in their footsteps.

Probably the most famous literary character associated with Seville is Don Juan. A bronze statue of the legendary lothario by sculptor Nicomedes Díaz Piquero (1936–2017) adorns the Plaza de Los Refinadores (Santa Cruz), where his story can be told.

The amorous conquests of Don Juan were first put to paper in 1630 in the play *El Burlador de Sevilla* (The Trickster of Seville) by the Spanish monk-cum-dramatist Tirso de Molina (1579–1648). Set in the 14th century, the three-act play is the earliest fully-developed dramatisation of the well-worn tale. In the first act our 'hero' declares his undying love to a duchess and then a peasant girl; in the second he seduces a nobleman's daughter, murdering her father when he is discovered; and in the third, he sweeps a bride off her feet much to the dismay of her groom. Only at the end does Don Juan get his comeuppance. The slain nobleman returns as a ghost, strikes Don Juan down thereby enabling his victims to resume their lives.

The legend of Don Juan has oft been retold, for example in the satirical comedy *Dom Juan* (1665) by Molière (1622–1673), the opera *Don Giovanni* by Mozart (1756–1791), and the play *Man and Superman* by George Bernard Shaw (1856–1950). Another is *Don Juan* by George Gordon, better known as Lord Byron (1788–1824), who arrived in Seville's *barrio* Santa Cruz in 1809. He stayed at a guesthouse on Calle Cruces (today Calle Fabiola 21) and in a playful twist, one probably inspired by the fact that his landlady took an amorous shine to him, he makes his protagonist the seduced rather than the seducer.

Yet another retelling is *Don Juan Tenorio* by the Spanish playwright José Zorrilla (1817–1893). His version includes elements from de Molina's original, as well as *Don Juan de Maraña* by Alexandre Dumas (1802–1870). A real-life inspiration for Zorrilla's version is the tiny Capilla de Nuestra Señora del Carmen on Calle Calatrava (La Macarena) in which he cloisters Don Juan's fiancée, the saintly Doña Inés.

Don Juan aside, Seville has inspired many other writers. The American Washington Irving (1783–1859) spent time here in the 1830s researching books on Columbus and the Alhambra. A wall plaque at Callejón del Agua 2 (Santa Cruz) marks the house where he lived. Another is the Englishman Somerset Maugham (1874–1965), who while penning his travelogue *The Land of the Blessed Virgin* lodged with the British vice-consul, at Calle Guzmán el Bueno 2.

A trio of Spanish authors concludes this survey. The world-famous novelist Miguel de Cervantes Saavedra (1547–1616) visited Seville twice, setting several of his *Novelas ejemplares* in the city. Numerous wall plaques (including one on Calle Sierpes) reference these works, with a bust at Calle Entre Cárceles 2 (Santa Cruz) marking the site of the royal

A statue of the legendary Don Juan in the Plaza de Los Refinadores

jail where he was wrongfully imprisoned. The Sevillian Luis Cernuda (1902–1963), who was born at Calle Acetres 6 (Santa Cruz), is remembered for *Orcnos*, a paean to the city written in exile during the Spanish Civil War. His work was informed by the poetry of the Sevillian Romanticist, Gustavo Adolfo Bécquer (1836–1870), to whom a monument is dedicated in the Parque de María Luisa.

Other locations nearby: 5, 6, 7, 9, 10, 11, 13

9   A Unique Place of Worship

Santa Cruz, the Iglesia de Santa María la Blanca at Calle Santa María la Blanca 5

There are more than 115 churches in Seville. Rich in historical interest, they provide a fascinating insight into Sevillian religious habits. Architecturally they range from Gothic–*Mudéjar* (Christian Moorish) through Renaissance to Baroque and beyond. Many were new builds at the time of construction although some rose on sites where mosques had stood. There is one, however, that uniquely bears witness to three different faiths: Islam, Judaism and Christianity. It is a reminder of the plurality *(convivencia)* that reigned in Seville before Christianity was fully reasserted.

The Iglesia de Santa María la Blanca stands at Calle Santa María la Blanca 5 (Santa Cruz), where recent renovation work has uncovered its remarkably long history (this could be even longer if the two columns from the Visigothic period (415–711 AD) on Calle Archeros are shown to come from a religious structure). Until then the earliest documented place of worship was a mosque constructed during Seville's long Moorish period (711–1248) although nothing remains except a few foundation stones and the memory.

Little of the synagogue that followed survives either although we know that approval for the mosque to be converted into a synagogue was given in 1252 by King Alfonso X (1221–1284). It was one of four synagogues that stood in the *Judería*, Seville's medieval Jewish quarter, and would have overlooked what was once the Jewish marketplace (see no. 10). Remarkably in the cellar of the café opposite, remains of the synagogue's ritual bath *(mikveh)* have been identified.

In 1391 following a pogrom against Seville's Jews, the synagogue was reworked as a Catholic church in the then-popular Gothic–*Mudéjar* style. During the 1660s, this building was demolished (except for the chancel) and a new church built in the Baroque style. Under the watchful eye of architect Juan González (1606–1674), a magnificent vault was installed over a tripartite nave, with a cupola on four pendentives. González also swapped up the original church columns for new ones carved from jasper quarried a hundred miles away in Antequera.

The exterior of the church, with its Gothic doorway (another survival of the original church), is austere except for a fancy belfry. Inside is a very different story. The vaults, arches and dome are smothered in decorative plasterwork courtesy of sculptor Pedro Roldán (1624–1699) and his brother Borja: geometric and floral motifs, cherubs and rosettes, even a representation of the Giralda. Together with wall murals, tiled dados and a painting of *La Cena* (The Last Supper) by Bartolomé Esteban *Murillo* (1617–1682), the whole is considered one of the jewels of Spanish Baroque (see no. 36). This wholesale deployment of flamboyant decoration by church authorities was a means of reassuring congregations after the social and economic upheaval brought about by the Black Death.

This stunning Baroque ceiling can be found inside the Iglesia de Santa María la Blanca

Several churches in Seville's La Macarena district also stand over demolished mosques. They include the sturdy Gothic–Mudéjar Iglesia de Santa Marina at Calle Sta. Marina 2A, one of Seville's oldest churches, dating from 1262. (see nos. 31, 34). Another, in the barrio Santa Cruz, is the Baroque Iglesia del Salvador on Plaza del Salvador, which contains part of a Moorish patio from Seville's very first mosque, its capitals typically salvaged from an older Roman building, and a bell tower resting on the base of its minaret.

Alongside these ruins one should not forget Seville's modern 30,000-strong Muslim community, which currently worships in a makeshift prayer hall on Plaza Ponce de León (La Macarena). Plans are afoot to construct a purpose-built mosque for them, the first in Seville for almost 800 years, using funds raised by veteran Seville footballer Frédéric Kanouté (b. 1977).

Other locations nearby: 5, 6, 7, 8, 9, 10, 11

10 Walking the Jewish Quarter

Santa Cruz, a walking tour of the former Judería starting at the¥Interpretation Centre for the Jewish Quarter of Seville (Centro de Interpretación Judería de Sevilla) at Calle Ximénez de Encisco 22

Jews first settled in Seville during the Roman period. They stayed on when Spain subsequently fell to the Catholic Visigoths and then the Moors. Only after 1248, when King Ferdinand III of Castile (1201–1252) reunited Seville with Christian Europe, did the lot of Seville's Jews change significantly.

From the Moorish period onwards, the Jews played an important economic role in city life. They occupied their own separate neighbourhood, the *Judería*, located just outside the Real Alcázar in today's *barrio* Santa Cruz. Here they not only received protection but also acted as a buffer between ruler and ruled in times of civil unrest. Surrounded by its own wall, the *Judería* contained synagogues, shops, schools, courts and a slaughterhouse.

After 1248 the Christian authorities allowed Jews to practise their faith although henceforth they were obliged to pay a special tax. During the reign of King Peter I (1334–1369) the community reached its height with around 6,000 inhabitants (roughly ten percent of the city's population). Prominent Jews were not only influential rabbis but also prominent merchants, scientists and physicians, and even held offices at the royal court.

This peaceful and plural period ended dramatically on the 6th of June 1391. Blamed for society's ills, the Jews were subjected to a pogrom sponsored by Church officials. Four thousand of them perished, with the survivors forcibly baptised. Thereafter King Henry III (1379–1406) gifted the *Judería* to his Chief Justice, with the Church also taking its share of the spoils. Streets were renamed, synagogues converted and all Jewish character erased. In 1481, the state-sponsored Inquisition executed many of the remaining Jews and by 1483 the few remaining had fled to North Africa. Having known Spain as *Sefarad* they were known thereafter as Sephardic Jews.

The starting point for a tour of what's left of Jewish Seville should be the Interpretation Centre for the Jewish Quarter of Seville (Centro de Interpretación Judería de Sevilla) at Calle Ximénez de Encisco 22. Here the story of the city's Jews is told using original artefacts and documents. Of particular interest is the painting *La expulsión de los judíos de Sevilla* by local historical artist Joaquin Turina y Areal (1847–1903).

Of the *Judería* itself, a tangle of small squares and alleys remains concealing several telling but hidden sights. Around the corner at Calle Fabiola 1–3, for example, stands the last remaining piece of wall that once enclosed the *Judería* (the millstones at the foot of the wall were incorporated to protect it from passing carriages). For an idea of how the old neighbourhood looked continue on to Dos Hermanos, an alley down the side of Calle Sta. María la Blanca 5, where a series of old courtyard houses have been converted into the Hotel Las Casas de La Judería. Of the former home of Seville's Jewish royal treasurer Samuel ha Leví (1320–1360) at Calle Levíes 4, an arcade is preserved at the Real Alcázar, and a fountain at the Casa de los Pinelo.

This solitary Jewish tomb can be found in an underground car park

Of the four synagogues in the *Judería* almost nothing remains. One of them, overlooking the former Jewish marketplace, was located alongside the Hotel Las Casas de La Judería, where the Church of Santa María la Blanca (Iglesia de Santa María la Blanca) stands today (see no. 9). Remarkably the synagogue's ritual bath *(mikveh)* has been identified in the cellar of the restaurant opposite. Other synagogues stood on the Plaza de Santa Cruz and Calle de San José.

One final location is the most poignant. In an underground car park on Calle Cano y Ceuto (parking bay 63 to be precise) there lurks a solitary brick tomb. It is all that remains of a Jewish cemetery that stood just beyond the wall of the *Judería*.

Other locations nearby: 6, 7, 8, 9, 11, 13

11 Three Small Galleries

Santa Cruz, Museo Bellver at Calle Fabiola 5

Three small but worthy art collections lie hidden in the streets of Santa Cruz. What makes them extra special is that the buildings containing them are also of interest. Two are grand Sevillian townhouses, whilst the third is a more modest former artist's home. All deserve the attention of those who enjoy their art in an intimate setting.

First is the Museo Bellver at Calle Fabiola 5. Like other townhouses from the 15th and 16th centuries, it gives little away from the outside other than a sturdy wooden door. By contrast, the inside of the building is a fine example of Spanish Renaissance, with a colonnaded *patio* and some magnificent ceilings. Known as the Casa Fabiola, it takes its name from the novel *Fabiola* (1854) by Nicholas Wiseman (1802–1865). Born here to Irish parents, Wiseman went on to become the first Archbishop of Westminster at a time when England's Roman Catholics had newly regained their legal status.

The house today forms a backdrop to the personal collection of Mariano Bellver (1927–2018), who spent most of his life in Seville indulging a passion for art and teaching (his grandfather, the sculptor Ricardo Bellver (1845–1924), created the tympanum relief of the Assumption at Seville Cathedral). Mariano's collecting began in 1960 and initially focussed on works from the Spanish Golden Age (1580–1680). This he later broadened to include 19th and 20th century *costumbrismo* canvasses. Depicting townscapes and everyday Andalucian life in colourful detail, these works were painted by members of the Seville School, including José García y Ramos (1852–1912), Antonio Cabral Bejarano (1798–1861) and José Dominguez Bécquer (1805–1841). Shortly before Bellver's death, the paintings were bequeathed together with sculptures, ceramics and furniture to the City of Seville, and the Casa Fabiola was purchased as the place in which to display them.

The second gallery, the Casa de los Pinelo, stands a couple of streets away at Calle Abades 7. It, too, is housed in a fine Renaissance townhouse. Centre stage is a lovely Andalucian courtyard or *patio* surrounded by a two-storey arcade formed from *Mudéjar* (Christian Moorish) arches smothered in ornate *plateresque* stucco (see no. 19). The *Mudéjar* idiom is also deployed to great effect on the ceilings.

Originally home to the Genoese Pinelo family, the house later served as a clerics' residence and then a hotel. Today it houses two cultural academies, which explains why visitors may encounter stu-

Porcelain and paintings at the Museo Bellver

dents going about their business. Both will appreciate not only the architecture but also the paintings and sculptures dotted here and there (look out for the matador's cape on which Picasso has added a signed sketch). Of particular interest is the collection of Chinese and Japanese art on the second floor. Donated in 2002 by Seville's Jesuit Society of Jesus (Compañía de Jesús), it is unique in Andalucia.

The third gallery is the former home and studio of the Granadino painter Amalio García del Moral y Garrido (1922–1995). Located in a corner of the lovely Plaza de Doña Elvira, the property was acquired by the artist in 1973 specifically for its unimpeded view of the Giralda, which he would "be able to contemplate (and) paint every day or night, in winter and summer". Just days before his death, Amalio created an eponymous foundation that subsequently restored the property and opened it to visitors. Visitors to the Museo Pintor Amalio can today visit and gaze through the window just as the artist did.

Other locations nearby: 7, 8, 9, 10, 12

12 The Home of Flamenco

Santa Cruz, the Flamenco Museum (Museo del Baile Flamenco)
at Calle Manuel Rojas Marcos 3

It has been said that nothing evokes *El duende* – that uniquely Spanish state of heightened emotion and expression – like *flamenco*. Based on the longstanding folk music traditions of Andalucia, this forcefully expressive art form embodies an authenticity that speaks of the joys and sorrows of human life. Largely neglected during the 1960s and 70s, recent years have seen a *flamenco* revival fuelled by interest from locals and visitors alike.

The exact origins of flamenco are hazy. The oldest record of *flamenco* music dates to 1774 in the book *Las Cartas Marruecas* (The Moroccan Letters), a survey of Spanish society by José Cadalso (1741–1782). Beyond that it is thought that *flamenco* developed sometime during the 16th century through cross-cultural interchange between *moriscos* (descendants of former Muslims converted to Christianity after the Reconquest) and *gitanos* (itinerant Roma people who arrived in Andalucia during the 15th century). Their hardship and alienation gave *flamenco* its sense of passion and yearning.

Flamenco comprises four key elements (excluding the venue, which can just as easily be a street corner as it can a stage). To the fore is always the dancer. A female dancer *(bailaora)* wears a swirling dress to emphasise her graceful turns: a male dancer *(bailaor)* sports trousers tailored to draw attention to his furious high-heeled footwork. Their soundtrack is provided by a *flamenco* guitarist *(tocaor)*, whose rolling strums are played on a lightweight instrument, with a board beneath the sound hole for tapping out the intricate rhythm. This is bolstered by a hand clapper-cum-singer *(cantaor)*, whose vibrating wail recalls the Muslim call to prayer. The aural experience is rounded out by the clicks of the castanets *(castañuelas)* played by the *bailaoras*.

Historians say that *flamenco* originated in eastern Andalucia but that hasn't stopped Sevillians claiming the art form for themselves. They will tell you it began in the working-class district of Triana, where their own Roma community was based until the 1970s, when it was uprooted and moved to the Las Tres Mil Viviendas housing estate on the southern edge of the city. Old habits die hard though and it is still said that children baptised in the Iglesia de Santa Ana, Seville's oldest parish church (1266), on Calle Pelay Correa, automatically receive the spirit of *flamenco*.

A lively performance at Seville's Flamenco Museum

Flamenco's official home in Seville today is the Flamenco Museum (Museo del Baile Flamenco) in the *barrio* Santa Cruz. Occupying a restored 18th century house at Calle Manuel Rojas Marcos 3, it provides visitors with an interactive introduction to the art form. In the upstairs art gallery don't miss the remarkable hand-cranked teaching machine with a pair of wooden shoes that tap out the various flamenco rhythms. This is much more than a museum though, since *flamenco* really comes alive here not only with a dance school but also a choreographed evening stage show (the latter are called *tablao* in reference to the wooden stage boards on which the dancers perform).

Many other venues in Seville offer *flamenco* shows. Some, like the Casa de la Memoria at Calle Cuna 6 (Santa Cruz), are full-blown *tablaos*. Others, known as *peñas*, offer a more intimate club setting, for example Peña Flamenca Torres Macarena at Calle Torrijiano 29 (La Macarena). With no strict choreography, the dancers here improvise their moves thereby making each performance unique.

In 2010, UNESCO declared *flamenco* one of its Masterpieces of the Oral and Intangible Heritage of Humanity. This accolade is celebrated in Seville's Bienal de Arte Flamenco festival held during the last two weeks in September in even-numbered years.

Other locations nearby: 3, 5, 11, 13, 18, 19

13 A Moorish Bath Revealed

Santa Cruz, Cervecería Giralda at Calle Mateos Gago 1

It was long thought that no Moorish-era bathhouses *(hammams)* survived in Seville, at least not beyond the shadowy remains of one in the basement of the Restaurante San Marco at Calle Mesón del Moro 6 (Santa Cruz). That view, however, changed recently with the discovery of two fine examples hidden in plain sight.

The finest was found unexpectedly in 2020, when renovation work at a popular *tapas* bar, Cervecería Giralda at Calle Mateos Gago 1, revealed a near-complete Almohad-era *hammam*. Dating back to the 12th century, it appears in Christian texts of 1281 not long after the Reconquest of Seville, when it is referred to as the Baths of García Jofre. By the 17th century, however, it was thought to have been demolished and the vaulted structure in its place was instead the relic of "some circus or amphitheatre". In actual fact it was the original bathhouse, now the premises of a merchant, its vaulted ceiling lowered, skylights blocked and columns replaced.

Fast forward now to the early 20th century and the building again changed function. This time the architect Vicente Traver y Tomás (1888–1966) converted it into a hotel and restaurant. He concealed the original bathhouse walls with plaster thereby saving them from further damage. It was these walls that reappeared unexpectedly during the recent renovation work.

Such bathhouses originally formed part of the Muslim purification ritual and were especially popular before running water was installed in private homes. Strongly associated with the Muslim countries of the Maghreb, as well as Ottoman-era Turkey, each comprised a series of hot and cold rooms used to relax the muscles and joints, stimulate the blood and tone the skin. The names of the various rooms are still those used in Roman times, namely Tepidarium (warm bath), Caldarium (hot bath) and Frigidarium (cold bath).

In the case of the bathhouse on Calle Mateos Gago, the Tepidarium occupied what is today the restaurant's main bar area. Measuring almost 22 feet square, it is covered with an octagonal vaulted ceiling resting on four slender columns. Of particular interest are the remains of geometric designs painted on the walls in red ochre (including rosettes and zig-zags representing water). Such high quality decoration covering the walls from top to bottom are unique for Moorish bathhouses in Spain.

To one side is a rectangular room measuring 13.5 by 42.5 feet, which once served as the Frigidarium. Here were found five rows of skylights, another unique feature among contemporary Moorish bathhouses, which at most have only three. In all eighty eight skylights have been revealed in varying shapes and sizes, including stars, octagons and rosettes. The present kitchen area is assumed to have been the Caldarium although of this only a single arch remains. The reason why this bathhouse was so grand was undoubtedly due to its close proximity to Seville's main mosque, which stood on the site of the present-day Cathedral.

This Moorish hammam was found recently in a busy tapas bar

The second Moorish *hammam* is more modest. Called the Baños de la Reina Mora, it stands at Calle Baños 17 (La Macarena) and also dates to the Almohad period, when Seville's city wall was extended northwards. The bathhouse was used until the 16th century, when it became part of a convent and then barracks. Now restored, it serves as a cultural venue.

For a modern takes on Roman and Moorish bathing rituals visit the Aire Ancient Baths at Calle Aire 15 and Las Termas de Hispalis at Calle Sta. María la Blanca 5 (both Santa Cruz). The latter name references that of Seville in Roman times.

Other locations nearby: 1, 2, 3, 4, 5, 6, 10, 11

14 The Pipes of Carmona

Outside Santa Cruz in the district of Nervión, the remains of the Caños de Carmona (Pipes of Carmona) aqueduct at the junction of Calle Luis Montoto and Calle José Maria Moreno Galván

Just outside Santa Cruz in the district of Nervión can be found the remains of an engineering marvel. At the start of Calle Luis Montoto stand two sturdy brick arcades with their ends abruptly shorn off. Now marooned on a busy road, they are fragments of a Roman aqueduct that once brought fresh water into Seville.

The aqueduct was originally built between 68 and 65 BC during the tenure of Julius Caesar (100–44 BC) as Roman provincial official *(quaestor)* of Hispania Ulterior. Contemporary with Seville's earliest city wall, it consisted of hundreds of arches on piers built mainly from bricks (see no. 37). The aqueduct was fed by a powerful spring in Alcalá de Guadaíra about 11 miles east of Seville, where a series of rock-cut and brick-built tunnels still mark the spot.

During the early 1170s, the aqueduct was overhauled and reworked on the initiative of the Almohad caliph Abu Yaqub Yusuf (1135–1184).

The remains of a Roman aqueduct on Calle Luis Montoto

As well as watering Seville, it now also watered the gardens and orchards of the Buhaira Palace, which Yusuf built between today's Bernardo and Nervión neighbourhoods.

Following the Reconquest of Seville by King Ferdinand III (1201–1252), the aqueduct was again renovated and by the late-14th century attained its maximum length. Old engravings clearly show it arriving at Seville's Puerta de Carmona, a city gate that once led to that particular town but which was demolished in 1868, and after which the aqueduct is named: Caños de Carmona (Pipes of Carmona). There it disgorged into a great cistern from where water was distributed across the city, primarily to religious and aristocratic establishments (notably the Real Alcázar), as well as royal orchards, flour mills, public fountains and baths. The prodigious flow is thought to have been around 1.3 million gallons a day.

By the late-19th century, however, the aqueduct's arches were doubling as shelters for criminals and vagrants. With piped water becoming more commonplace, and plans afoot for Seville's suburban enlargement, the decision was taken to demolish the aqueduct. It was a sign of the times that the historic structure was deemed by Madrid's Monuments Commission "a vulgar work, without artistic features, devoid of archaeological interest".

Demolition began in January 1912 although it took until 1959 for the last remaining sections to be cleared to make way for the new districts of La Candelaria and Los Pajaritos. Fortunately, during the demolition process three short, five-arched sections were left standing. The section at the start of Calle Luis Montoto survived by being incorporated into the piers of the Puente de la Calzada railway bridge erected in 1930. It reappeared in 1991, when the bridge was dismantled and the railway lines removed. Remarkably elderly Catholics today brave the rushing traffic to venerate a tiled picture of the Virgin Mary installed in one of the arches!

The second section stands a short distance farther east on the corner with Calle Jiménez Aranda. It was spared because it stood in a private orchard obligating the demolition team to pass it by. A fascinating old photo of the aqueduct hereabouts shows it crossing the now-vanished Tagarete River, which once skirted the old city walls before emptying into the Guadalquivir alongside the Torre del Oro.

The third and final section stands a mile and a quarter father east on Calle Cigüeña. It was saved on the initiative of preservationist Carlos Serra y Pickman, a member of Seville's influential Pickman family.

Other locations nearby: 9, 15

15 Palaces for the New Rome

Santa Cruz, the Casa de Pilatos at Plaza de Pilatos 1

In 1248, King Ferdinand III of Castile (1201–1252) wrested Seville from the Moors bringing an end to 500 years of Muslim rule. The Castilian aristocracy, which had assisted in the so-called *Reconquista*, was rewarded with land on which to build palatial homes. Such was their grandeur that Seville was dubbed 'The New Rome'.

Moorish influence, however, persisted in architecture long after the Reconquest. Christian monarchs, notably Alfonso X (1221–1284) and Peter I (1334–1369), retained Muslim artisans to build palaces and churches. Known as *Mudéjares* – from the Arabian *mudajjan* meaning 'those permitted to stay' – they synthesised Islamic and Christian forms to create the distinct *Mudéjar* style.

A blueprint for the style was provided by Seville's Real Alcázar, the palace-fortress built by the Moors and later converted into a Christian royal residence (see no. 1). Here the sensible Moorish arrangement of rooms overlooking a private courtyard – with shaded ground floor rooms used in summer and warmer ones above in winter – was retained. Much of the flamboyant Moorish decoration was kept, too, including horseshoe-shaped arches, intricate plasterwork, and polychrome glazed tiles *(azulejos)*. To these the Christians added Gothic and Renaissance elements, as well as Classical statuary.

By the 16th century, with wealth pouring into Seville from the New World, the city's oligarchs wanted *Mudéjar* palaces of their own. A fine example is the Casa de Pilatos at Plaza de Pilatos 1 (Santa Cruz). Construction was initiated in 1483 by Pedro Enríquez de Quiñones (d. 1493), Governor of Andalucia, and completed by his son Fadrique Enríquez de Rivera (1476–1539), Marquess of Tarifa. In 1521, following a tour of the Holy Land, Fadrique created a *Via Crucis* (Way of Cross) from the palace to a point outside Seville's walls. The 1,321 steps mimicked those said to have separated the praetorium of Pontius Pilate, the Roman governor who ordered Jesus' crucifixion, and Calvary, where the execution took place. The novel conceit eventually gave rise to the name Casa de Pilatos.

Fadrique's tour also took in Italy, where the Renaissance was in full swing. Suitably impressed he commissioned Genoese sculptor Antonio María Aprile (1500–1550) to design a Renaissance-style Carrara marble entrance to his palace. Beyond is a typical Andalucian *Patio Principal* or main courtyard. It has a fountain in the centre surrounded by two-storey *Mudéjar* arcades topped with Gothic balustrades. The arcades are decorated with *azulejos*, Roman and Greek statues, and busts of Spanish kings. This heady concoction is taken further in adjacent chambers, notably the Salón del Pretorio, with its coffered heraldic ceiling, and the chapel, with its Gothic rib vaults.

From the courtyard a magnificent tiled stairway with an ornate wooden *media naranja* (half orange) dome leads upstairs. The rooms here contain antiques, furniture and paintings by a variety of artists from the 16th century onwards, including a *Pietà* by Venetian artist Sebastiano del Piombo (1485–1547).

Outside in the garden once stood an urn said to contain the ashes of the Roman Emperor Trajan. Cinema buffs may like to know that the palace features in David Lean's *Lawrence of Arabia* (1962), as well as Ridley Scott's *1492: Conquest of Paradise* (1992).

Classical meets Mudéjar at the Casa de Pilatos

Seville's other *Mudéjar* palaces include the Palacio de Lebrija at Calle Cuna 8, with its collection of artefacts from the Roman city of Itálica, the Casa de Salinas at Calle Mateos Gago 39, with arches smothered in *Plateresque* plasterwork, the Palacio Marqueses de la Algaba on Plaza Calderón de la Barca, which contains a museum of *Mudéjar* art, and the Palacio de las Dueñas at Calle Dueñas 5 (see no. 32). Something rather special is the Palacio de Santa Coloma at Calle Santa Clara 23 (La Macarena). Built for a noble family in the 17th century, it is rendered in what is locally termed *barroco sosegado* or 'quiet Baroque', its austere street façade giving away nothing of the lovely Renaissance patio within. Today it is divided into two, with part of it taken up by the Palacio Bucarelli hotel accessible at Calle de la Dalia 1.

Other locations nearby: 14, 16

16   A Courtyard Full of Neighbours

Santa Cruz, the Corral del Conde at Calle Santiago 27 (note: the main door is kept locked so it is best to ask one of the residents politely for a look)

Calle Santiago in the *barrio* Santa Cruz holds a secret. Half way along this narrow street there is a stern, whitewashed façade broken only by a few small windows and a sturdy door. Easily overlooked, or even mistaken for a prison, it conceals a traditional Sevillian residential complex. The Corral del Conde is acknowledged as Seville's oldest and most complete example of a *corral de vecinos* or neighbourhood compound.

The *corral* concept originated in Moorish times, when extended families occupied rooms ranged around an internal courtyard, shielded from the dusty street by a blank wall. During the 16th century, when New World wealth began swelling Seville's population, these *corrales* grew in size, too. They were usually home to the working classes, notably builders, blacksmiths, carpenters and cobblers. An artisan and his family inhabited a single room, with communal washing and cooking facilities available in the courtyard. This made *corrales* an affordable albeit overcrowded place to live.

Today many *corrales* have been swept away. This makes the Corral del Conde special and yet it rarely appears in tourist literature. The reason is probably because it gives so little away from the outside (there is only a miniscule nameplate over the doorway) and getting inside is difficult. Access to what is a private residence is by buzzer only, so visitors should respectfully bide their time until a willing resident affords them a glimpse (a notice inside states that visitors should be quiet).

The name Corral del Conde reflects the fact that it was originally owned by Gaspar de Guzmán, Count–Duke (Conde) of Olivares (1587–1645), a member of one of Spain's oldest noble families. Remarkably since his time the basic layout of the *corral* has survived intact: a cobbled courtyard with fountain, three-storey residential ranges with wooden galleries, a laundry room, bread oven and chapel.

Following a long overdue renovation in 1982, the seventy or so rooms (reduced from an original 113) have been popular with artists, young couples and the occasional holidaymaker. With its trees and potted plants, the place has a peaceful air about it. Back in the 16th

A 19th-century engraving of life in the Corral del Conde

century, however, these same rooms would have housed a dozen or more people each. The thought of a thousand people all talking, cooking and washing makes for a very different scene!

A constant throughout has been the fountain, which as well as being used for washing would also have been used in family celebrations such as baptisms, for commercial trades and holy vigils. It can be seen clearly in old photographs from the 19th century, with women doing their laundry and long lines of drying clothes suspended from the galleries. One missing element is the caretaker *(casera)*, who would have lived alongside the main door. Not only did he vet visitors but he also collected rents and mediated in disputes between neighbours.

It is worth remembering that access to the *corral* is also possible during Easter Holy Week (Semana Santa), when some of the city's church brotherhoods *(cofradias)* visit the chapel. Failing that, a sense of the *corral's* size can be gained simply by walking the rest of its perimeter wall along Calle Ave María and Calle Azafrán.

A couple of more modest *corrales* are worth finding in Triana. Until the 1970s, the Corral de la Encarnación at Calle Pagés del Corro 130 and the Corral de las Flores at Calle Castilla 16 were both occupied by the district's Roma community.

Other locations nearby: 15, 33

17 Old Fashioned Commerce

Santa Cruz, a tour of some traditional shops including the clothier Juan Foronda at Calle Sierpes 33

Walk along Calle Sierpes in the *barrio* Santa Cruz and it will be apparent how much Sevillians enjoy their shopping. Moreover, they prefer 'real' shops rather than the faceless suburban malls that have decimated city centres elsewhere. This has helped preserve something of the city's traditional commercial landscape, as well as a healthy number of independent specialist stores.

Calle Sierpes has long been an important centre of trade. Once lined with blacksmiths, cobblers and other artisans, much of it is today pedestrianised, where international brands rub shoulders with venerable local names. In the summertime, awnings *(cortinas de sombre)* are strung from the rooftops to provide shade, and street performers entertain locals taking their evening stroll *(paseo)*. Always bustling, Calle Sierpes is at its liveliest in the run up to Easter, when it forms part of the processional route for Holy Week (Semana Santa).

This short tour of traditional shops begins with La Campana at Calle Sierpes 1–3. Founded in 1888, this is Seville's best-known *pastelería* (cake shop). One end of the shop is taken up with a confectionery counter, its shelves loaded with freshly-made *yemas* (orange and egg yolk sweets), *lenguas de almendra* (Moorish-style almond pastries), candied fruits and *primor de hojaldre* (puff pastries). At the other end is a bar where locals congregate for tea and pastries *(merienda)*. No wonder there is a vintage weighing machine in one corner!

Next stop is Papeleríe Ferrer at number 5. Spain's oldest stationer, it was opened in 1856 by a Catalan couple who paused in Seville en route to America. Greeted with immediate success they stayed put and their shop, with its original countertops, remains unchanged. Slightly younger is watchmaker Enrique Sanchis at 19–21. Established in 1901 by a family from eastern Spain, it features six large clocks on the façade, installed for the Ibero–American Exposition of 1929 (Exposición iberoamericana de 1929).

Juan Foronda at number 33 is the place women go for Andalucian dress accessories. Worn at weddings, *ferias*, bullfights and funerals, these include tasselled lace shawls *(mantones)* (including *mantoncillos* hand-embroidered with flowers), white and black lace veils *(mantillas)* worn with high tortoiseshell combs *(peinas)*, hand-painted fans *(abanicos)*, and castanets *(castañuelas)*. For wide-brimmed gents'

Fans for sale at Juan Foronda on Calle Sierpes

sombreros cordobés visit the milliner Maquedano at number 40, where traditional headwear has been made to measure since 1908. Another long-established shop selling traditional clothing is Diaz at number 71.

One's sense of old-fashioned commerce is enhanced by several other sights nearby. These include some wonderful tiled wall advertisements, most notably a near life-sized one from 1924 at Calle Tetuán 9 promoting Studebaker automobiles (others endorse *La Gitana* cigars, *Caballero* brandy and *Exquisitos Cafés Seleccionados* coffee) (see inside back cover). The Pedro Roldán Building on Plaza de Jesus de la Pasion was built in 1925 to a design by local commercial architect José Espiau y Muñoz (1879–1938) for a textile company and features a tiled neo-Moorish façade (back in medieval times this square hosted Seville's bakers' market). A little farther away at Calle Marcos 38, there is Cordoneria–Alba, a traditional braid and tassle maker in business since 1904.

Of interest here is the Real Círculo de Labradores at the junction of Calle Sierpes and Calle Pedro Caravaca. This private members' club founded in 1859 by aristocratic landowners has long prided itself in providing a discreet bolthole for Seville's commercial and professional elite. The prefix 'Real' (royal) was approved in 1917 by King Alfonso XIII (1886–1941), who ratified the club's statutes.

Other locations nearby: 18, 29

18   Chocolate and Churros

It is well documented that the greatest European consumer of chocolate is the small, dairy-rich country of Switzerland. Remarkably the Swiss consume 19.8 pounds of chocolate per head of population annually. The British are placed second with 15 pounds, whereas the Spanish eat just 7.5 pounds. Despite this lower ranking, it is Spain that lays claim to first exposing Europe to chocolate.

A good place to reflect on Spain's role in the chocolate story is the family-run Bar El Comercio at Calle Lineros 9 (Santa Cruz). This busy little *tapas* bar has been serving up cups of thick hot chocolate since 1904, and is still in the hands of the founding Rivera family. Each cup is traditionally accompanied by a pile of fried, unsweetened dough strips known as *churros*, which are perfect for dipping in hot chocolate. *Chocolate con churros* is traditionally consumed between breakfast *(desayuno)* and late morning, and then again later in the afternoon. At Bar El Comercio it can be enjoyed either on the premises or else as a takeaway, and in half or full portions.

It was Spanish and Portuguese explorers *(conquistadors)* who brought chocolate to Europe more than 500 years ago. Christopher Columbus (1451–1506) is credited with being the first European to encounter cocoa beans, when he intercepted a trading vessel during his fourth voyage. Believing the cargo to be almonds, however, he ignored it leaving the real discovery to Hernan Cortés (1485–1547). Cortés was famously mistaken in Mexico for a god and initiated into the ritual feasts of the Aztecs, where he was treated to a bitter, peppery cocoa drink called *Tchocolatl*. Realising its potential as a commercial product, he brought the first cocoa beans to Europe in the name of the Spanish crown.

Once in Spain, the art of turning cocoa beans into drinking chocolate was entrusted to Cistercian monks. During the 16th century they manufactured the novel drink for the Spanish nobility, and with Spain's monopoly on the import of cocoa beans, the formula remained a state secret for over a century. The monks also made drinking chocolate more palatable by swapping Mexican peppers for sugar cane from the Canary Islands. This reworked drink was served hot instead of the lukewarm version favoured in the Americas.

Only during the 17th century as the Spanish Empire faltered did the country's hold on chocolate weaken. So the fashion for drinking

Chocolate and churros at Bar El Comercio

chocolate spread to France and Italy, where it remained the preserve of the upper classes. It remained this way until the 1820s, when a Dutch chemist discovered a way to make powdered chocolate. This paved the way for a British company to manufacture the first chocolate bar bringing the once exclusive and expensive product to the masses in an affordable and portable format.

There are plenty of other *Churreria* in Seville serving good *Chocolate con churros*. Aficionados recommend La Centuria at Plaza de la Encarnación 8 (La Macarena), Bar El Pilar at Avenida de José Laguillo 2 (just outside La Macarena), and Chocolatería Virgen de Luján at Calle Virgen del Águila 2 (Triana).

Should one ever tire of *churros* then chocolate in Seville is also available in many other forms. These include everything from straightforward bars of dark chocolate filled with nuts to *Palmera de Chocolate* (pastry hearts dipped in chocolate) and *Napolitana de Chocolate* (chocolate-filled puff pastry pockets). These can be found in most good cake shops *(pastelería)* (see no. 17).

Other locations nearby: 12, 17, 19, 20, 21

19 Like a Giant Silver Box

Santa Cruz, the Town Hall (Ayuntamiento) at Plaza Nueva 1
(note: guided tours only Monday to Thursday 4.30 and 7.30pm,
and Saturday 10am)

As its name suggests, Plaza Nueva is one of Seville's newer public squares. Completed in 1856, it is overlooked on three sides by later structures. Only on the fourth side is the pattern broken by the much older Town Hall (Ayuntamiento). To fully appreciate this magnificent building one should view it first from the front on Plaza de San Francisco.

The Town Hall, or Casa Consistorial (Council Meeting Room), was constructed in 1526 to mark the marriage of Holy Roman Emperor and King of Spain Charles V (1500–1558) to Isabella of Portugal (1503–1539). Such a powerful union warranted a representative council building, one that reflected the power and influence of Golden Age Seville. Accordingly, the Town Hall's frontage was rendered in the then fashionable Renaissance style by architect Diego de Riaño (d. 1534). It was suitably adorned with reliefs representing not only the king but also Julius Caesar and Hercules, Seville's Roman and legendary founders respectively. Of particular interest is the richly-carved stonework around the doors and windows. Peculiar to Spanish architecture between the Late Gothic and Renaissance periods, it is known as *Plateresque* decoration. From the word *platero* meaning silversmith, the decoration does indeed resemble embossed silverwork. From afar it gives the building the appearance of a giant silver trinket box.

At the time of the Town Hall's construction the rear of the building was unadorned since it backed directly onto the Convento de San Francisco. Built in 1270, the convent remained operational until 1840, when it was demolished following damage by Napoleonic troops (it is interesting to note that long before the convent this area was part of the Guadalquivir river, which explains the Roman pilings, 6th century anchor and 10th century ship unearthed here in the 1980s). The unadorned rear was eventually rendered in the neo-Classical style following the construction of the Plaza Nueva.

Inside the Town Hall, on the lower floor, there can be found some original sculptured ceilings, including that of the chapter house, which depicts various Spanish monarchs. On the first floor, the upper chapter house features a magnificent gilded wooden ceiling (*alfarje*) and paint-

Plateresque decoration on Seville's Town Hall

ings by Baroque masters Francisco de Zurbarán (1598–1664) and Juan de Valdés Leal (1622–1690).

Of the other buildings facing Plaza Nueva it is worth noting the neo-Baroque Telefónica building (1926) by Juan Talavera y Heredia (1880–1960) at number 2 and the tiny Capilla de San Onofre next door, the only part remaining of the old convent. In the centre of the square is an equestrian statue of King Ferdinand III (1201–1252), who wrested Seville from the Moors in 1248, an action for which he was canonised in 1671.

Above the Town Hall's *Plateresque* window frames can be seen the curious inscription NO8DO. This is a rebus, a literary device whereby a phrase is represented cryptically by letters and figures. In this case the phrase is *No me ha dejado* (She (Seville) has not abandoned me), with the '8' figuratively representing a skein of wool *(madeja)*. The phrase was said to have been coined by King Alfonso X (1221–1284) in reference to Seville's support when his second son Sancho (1258–1295) attempted to usurp him. The NO8DO rebus can also be found on Seville's municipal flag, the tomb of Christopher Columbus in Seville Cathedral, and even the city's iron manhole covers (see page 120). The main façade also includes stone reliefs of Grace Kelly and Orson Welles added during building renovations. See if you can spot them.

Other locations nearby: 3, 12, 18, 20, 21

20   An Architect Leaves His Mark

El Arenal, a tour of buildings designed by Aníbal González including several residential buildings on Avenida de la Constitución

Few architects have left a mark on a city like Aníbal González (1876–1929). Born in Seville, he studied architecture in Madrid, where in 1902 he graduated with top marks. Immediately afterwards he married into a family of architects and established a practice of his own. Despite having been thus far exposed to revivalist Historicism, his first twenty or so projects in Seville were all Modernist in style. They include an electricity sub-station (1906) at Calle Feria 154 and a fabric factory (1909) at the junction of Calle Torneo and Calle Lumbreras (La Macarena). Both show a preference for materials and function over ornamentation.

In 1909 González suddenly switched his focus from Modernism back to Historicism. Two years later he won a competition to become Director of Works for Seville's Ibero–American Exposition of 1929 (Exposición iberoamericana de 1929). With a brief to celebrate the past achievements of Spain and its former colonies in a World's Fair-style event, González deemed Historicism the perfect idiom in which to work.

Although the event was not scheduled to take place until 1929, there was much to be done. It was proposed that a series of grand pavilions be erected on land south of the city centre. Once the gardens of the Palacio de San Telmo, the land was willed to the city by the Infanta María Luisa Fernanda (1832–1897). Named Parque de María Luisa in her honour, it was landscaped by Frenchman Jean Claude Nicolas Forestier (1861–1930). This created a verdant backdrop against which González built his pavilions, which were originally connected by a miniature railway.

González's brand of Historicism embraced neo-Gothic, neo-Renaissance and most famously neo-*Mudéjar* in which he revived earlier Christian Moorish forms, themselves derived from genuine Moorish architecture (see no. 15). He deployed these using Andalucian materials and construction techniques such as exposed brickwork, glazed ceramics *(azulejos)* and wrought iron giving rise to the term Sevillian Regionalism or *Andalucismo*.

All these elements were deployed by González in three Exposition pavilions clustered around the Plaza de América: the Mudéjar Pavilion (Pabellón Mudéjar), the neo-Renaissance Fine Arts Pavilion (Pabellón de Bellas Artes) and the neo-Gothic Royal Pavilion (Pabellón Real) (see nos. 50, 51). They are only overshadowed by González's Plaza de España, a jaw-dropping exercise in Historicism that served as the headquarters of the host nation and the Exposition's focal point (see no. 53).

Tragically in 1926 González fell foul of the Exposition committee and resigned. He died impoverished aged fifty-three just days after the Exposition opened. Despite this, his eclectic designs continue to enliven Seville to this day, much to the delight of many visitors. Tthey comprise more than a hundred Historicist projects, the majority of them residential. Typical is the flamboyant neo-*Mudéjar* house at

An apartment house on Avenida de la Constitución by Aníbal González

the corner of Calle Sta. María de Gracia and Calle Martín Villa (La Macarena). Corner buildings were a González speciality and another can be found at Avenida de la Constitución 14, with its eye-catching turret stairwell. More buildings by González can be found in the same block at numbers 12, 10 and 6. The extravagant corner building La Adriática at number 2 (together with its twin, Ciudad de Londres, at Calle Cuna 30) is by José Espiau y Muñoz (1879–1938), an architect clearly influenced by the work of Aníbal González.

The Exposition of 1929 kickstarted urban improvements well beyond Parque de María Luisa. Standard lamps and fountains were erected in Seville's city centre, new neighbourhoods were built to the south, and sporting facilities created, including the first incarnation of the Benito Villamarín Football Stadium in Heliópolis.

Other locations nearby: 2, 3, 5, 19, 21, 22

21   A Handful of Historic Bars

El Arenal, a selection of historic bars including Casa Moreno at Calle Gamazo 7

Seville boasts more than a few historic bars each with a story to tell. Take El Rinconcillo in La Macarena, which lays claim not only to being the city's oldest bar but also the place where *tapas* were invented (see no. 33). Casa Cuesta in Triana may be younger but it still packs a historical punch, with its vintage tiled wall advertisements and bullfighting posters (see no. 46). What follows is a further selection of historic bars in Seville.

We begin with Casa Moreno at Calle Gamazo 7 (El Arenal). Once upon a time it was commonplace in Seville for shops to double as bars. From the 1960s onwards, however, as retail habits changed, these so-called *abacerías* began dying out. Today only a few remain and Casa Moreno is a fine example. The premises are cramped, which might put the casual visitor off but rest assured the welcome is warm and the experience memorable. At the front is the shop selling all sorts of cured meats, cheeses and conserves. Through an archway beyond is the bar, which consists of a long metal-topped counter. Here regulars stand casually enjoying small open-faced sandwiches known as *montaditos*, which are washed down with a glass of *fino* sherry, wine or beer.

Also in El Arenal is Casa Morales. Established in 1850, this is now more of a fully-fledged bar and restaurant than the hybrid *abacería* it once was. It does, however, still retain its bipartite design. The bar is accessed at Calle García de Vinuesa 11, where locals stand at tall tables sipping sherry and nibbling olives. The wooden bar and fretwork shelving add to the traditional feel. Around the corner on Calle Cristóbal de Castillejo is the restaurant, which originally functioned as a retail winery. The towering terracotta wine vats serve today as poster boards.

Another bar in El Arenal that offers authenticity is Bodeguita Romero at Calle Harinas 10. It opened in 1939 in the Mercado de Encarnación but when that was closed (later to be replaced by the Metropol Parasol) it relocated to its current address. Still run by the same family, it offers good quality *tapas* as well as some great sandwiches, including local favourite *Montadito de Pringá* made from leftover stew.

This tour continues in La Macarena with Casa Ricardo at Calle Hernán Cortés 2. Opened in 1898 and revamped over the years, the bar retains its traditional atmosphere. Notably, given the pious nature of

Casa Moreno on Calle Gamazo
is one of the last abacerías

La Macarena, its walls are covered with religious images thereby mix-
ing drinking and devotion in a manner typical of Seville. Also in this
area is Antigua Abaceria de San Lorenzo, an eclectic restaurant-cum-
grocery store at Calle Teodosio 53.

We finish in the *barrio* Santa Cruz with Alvaro Peregil La Goleta at
Calle Mateos Gagos 20. Little more than a shuttered hole-in-the-wall, it
was opened in 1904 as a wine shop by the current owner's grandfather.
He introduced *Vino de Naranja* to Seville from the city of Huelva and
jugs of the orange-flavoured white wine are still served there today.

For a modern take on the historic Seville bar, one should try the city's El Patio chain.
Of particular interest is the branch at Calle San Eloy 9 (El Arenal), with its casks of
sherry, sandwiches stacked high, and great trays of *tapas*. To the rear is a tiled, stepped
seating area, which gets positively riotous during public holidays, when it seems the
entire neighbourhood descends on the place.

Other locations nearby: 2, 3, 19, 22, 23, 26

22   Plazas and Patios

El Arenal, a selection of *plazas* and *patios* including the Plaza del Cabildo off Avenida de la Constitución

Seville's Old Town (Casco Antiguo) comprises a tangle of narrow streets opening onto public squares (*plazas*). This layout was dictated not only by the limited space available within the city walls but also by the weather. Narrow streets guaranteed shade and *plazas* were often adorned with orange trees and fountains to mitigate the heat of the sun. Well-to-do homes boasted their own private *plazas* in the form of an internal courtyard or *patio*, which might also contain plants and water features. Together *plazas* and *patios* are a defining feature of traditional Seville.

A unique *plaza* is the Plaza del Cabildo reached by means of a covered passage opposite the cathedral on Avenida de la Constitución (El Arenal). Unlike most *plazas*, which are rectilinear, this one is semi-circular. Its flat side is formed by a well-preserved stretch of Seville's old city wall (see no. 37). The curved side is formed by an arcade that sits over the demolished San Miguel College, once part of the cathedral. Above this rise three further storeys added during the 1930s. What makes the whole especially attractive are the partial vaults (known as pendentives) reaching inwards from the arcade to support a balustraded walkway, and again to support the tiled roof. Painted decoration on these vaults contrasts nicely with the whitewash used across the rest of the structure. The *plaza* attracts visitors and locals alike, who not only attend its Sunday collectors' market but also a shop selling *yemas* (sweets made with egg yolks, sugar and orange peel) produced by the nuns of Seville's closed convents. The shop is called El Torno after the revolving wall drum used by the nuns to exchange goods without being seen.

The collectors' market previously took place in the tiny but more typical Plaza Santa Marta. Hidden at the end of an alley behind a statue of Pope John Paul II in the Plaza Virgen de Los Reyes (Santa Cruz), it features a simple Cross and near-permanent shade. Another hidden example is the Plaza de la Escuela de Cristo, which can be reached by means of an alley at Calle Ximénez de Enciso 17.

Larger but also more typical is the triangular Plaza de San Leandro (Santa Cruz). At its southern end is the late-16th century closed Convento de San Leandro, where *yemas* are again sold through a discreet *torno* (see no. 34). The whitewashed convent buildings stand in quiet contrast to the 18th century Iglesia San Ildefonso opposite, which sports a colourfully-painted neo-Classical façade. The surrounding maze of alleys is worth exploring in their own right.

The Andalucian *patio* originated in Moorish times, when extended families occupied shaded rooms ranged around an internal courtyard screened from the street. Seville's finest examples are preserved in the city's numerous palaces open to the public (see nos. 1, 15). But even domestic *patios* are a joy to behold if their proud owners leave their doors ajar. A casual stroll along Calle San Vincente (El Macarena), for example, provides fleeting glimpses of

The Plaza del Cabildo is a unique Sevillian courtyard

some good examples, adorned with potted plants, fountains and religious effigies (properties that aren't blessed with a *patio* sometimes paint one on their garage door!). More *patios* can be found in the old aristocratic townhouses of the *barrio* Santa Cruz, for example at Callejón del Agua 2 and Calle Guzmán el Bueno 4 (see no. 7).

Visitors to Seville will often find a *patio* included as part of their accommodation (see no. 55). A nice example is the Casa Palacio San Isidoro, which occupies a former convent at Calle San Isidoro 5 (Santa Cruz).

Other locations nearby: 2, 3, 20, 21, 23, 25

23 A Medieval Shipyard

El Arenal, the Royal Shipyard of Seville (Reales Atarazanas de Sevilla) on Calle Temprado (note: the shipyard is currently being restored and is expected to reopen to visitors in 2024)

One of Seville's architectural gems lies hidden in plain sight. The medieval Royal Shipyard of Seville (Reales Atarazanas de Sevilla) fills an entire city block in El Arenal but has long been closed to visitors. This unique structure is now in the process of being restored and reopened.

The story of the shipyard goes back to 1248, when King Ferdinand III of Castile (1201–1252) wrested Seville from the Moors. To consolidate his position, and to secure the Straits of Gibraltar against the Moors' return, he needed ships and and a shipyard to build them. Following Ferdinand's death in 1252, his son Alfonso X (1221–1284) completed the yard and built a fleet.

The shipyard was erected between the city walls and the Guadalquivir River. Covering an area of 3.33 acres and bounded by today's Calle Temprado, Calle Almirantazgo, Calle Dos de Mayo and Calle Tomás de Ibarro, it consisted of seventeen brick-vaulted sheds. Each was large enough for the construction of a galley and set perpendicular to the sandy riverbank to facilitate easy launching (*El Arenal* means 'the sandy area').

It is documented that ten galleys were built in the shipyard's first year, and fleets of up to thirty vessels continued to be constructed for the remainder of the Reconquest, which only ended in 1492 when the Iberian Peninsula was entirely Christianised. After this, however, orders for new galleys dried up and the shipyard was partially repurposed. In 1493, for example, a fish market opened in one of the sheds. Later, during the 16th century, some sheds became storage depots for oil, wool, spices and mercury (for the extraction of silver), with others converted into customs warehouses *(aduana)*. The oil depot is recalled in the Postigo del Aceite (Oil Gate) on Calle Almirantazgo, one of four old city gates still extant (see no. 37).

By the 17th century, the sheds had become too small to accommodate modern vessels and shipbuilding ceased altogether (the shipyard was subsequently relocated downstream to Los Astilleros, where it has operated ever since). Then in 1674 at the instigation of local aristocrat Miguel de Mañara (1627–1679), a member of the Brotherhood of the Holy Charity (Hermandad de la Santa Caridad), five of the empty sheds became the Hospital de la Caridad. Occupied to this

Inside the Royal Shipyard of Seville

day by Seville's elderly, the building attracts visitors with its Baroque church, arcaded *patios* and surprisingly ghoulish paintings by Juan de Valdés Leal (1622–1690).

Later still, in 1719, seven sheds were given over to the storage of artillery munitions (the so-called Real Maestranza de Arteleria), with the rest used for commercial warehousing. This iteration remained in place until 1945, when the commercial warehouses were torn down to make way for Seville's new Tax Office (Delegación de Hacienda). Thereafter the now-disused artillery warehouses were given National Monument status henceforth protecting them from demolition.

What then to do with the remaining sheds? Different proposals came and went until late 2018, when it was decided to restore and open the unique structure to the public, with the unveiling scheduled for 2024 (should access still prove difficult, an open window on Calle Dos de Mayo might afford a glimpse). One happy group of visitors will be fans of the popular television series *Game of Thrones*. The shipyard sheds were used in Season 7, when they doubled as the cellars beneath the Red Keep, where Qyburn and Cersei shoot a bolt through the skull of the dragon Balerion.

Other locations nearby: 1, 2, 4, 22, 24, 25

24 The Tower of Gold

El Arenal, the Torre del Oro on Paseo de Cristóbal Colón

The discovery in 1492 of the Americas for Europe by Christopher Columbus (1451–1506) helped finance Spain's Golden Age. For much of the 16th century, the inland port of Seville held a monopoly on trade with the New World, and it was here that treasure fleets returned laden with loot and precious commodities. The ships' captains knew they were home when they spotted a sturdy tower, the Torre del Oro, on the banks of the Guadalquivir River.

The Torre del Oro still stands. Its distinctive tripartite structure – two crenelated dodecagonal drums surmounted by a domed cylinder – spans 500 years of the city's history. The lowest drum is the oldest part, constructed around 1220 by the Moorish governor of Seville, Abù l-Ulà (Seville at the time was part of the Almohad Caliphate). Its Arabic name *burj adh-dhahab* (Tower of Gold) was inspired by tiles once attached to its façade that reflected the sun onto the river. The name stuck and eventually inspired the tower's present name.

The tower's purpose was two-fold. Firstly, it served as a defensive forward lookout post or *albarrana*. A stand-alone bastion connected to the main wall by a bridge, it could easily be abandoned if overrun by enemies. Secondly, it provided an anchor point for a heavy chain suspended across the river to deter enemy ships. This was deployed in 1248 during the city's defence against the Castilian fleet. Eventually it was broken by Captain Ramón de Bonifaz (1196–c.1252) leading to the Reconquest of Seville.

The second level of the tower was constructed in the 14th century by King Peter I (1334–1369), who used the tower as a treasury. Narrower than the lowest level, it gives the tower its stepped profile. This is reinforced by the third and uppermost level designed in 1760 by Brussels-born military engineer Sebastián Van der Borcht (1725–??), who also designed the lantern crowning Seville Cathedral's Royal Chapel (Capilla Real). It is a reminder of the tower's function as a lookout. At the same time, the present main access was installed and the base of the tower reinforced with mortared rubble. Fortunately, later proposals to demolish the tower to make way for horse-drawn carriages approaching the Triana Bridge were refused by the king.

Since then, the tower has served a number of purposes, including a prison, chapel and harbourmaster's office. Currently it houses a maritime museum (Museo Marítimo) containing old navigational instru-

The Torre del Oro is one of Seville's foremost Moorish survivals

ments, sea charts and other artefacts pertaining to Seville's time as one of the richest ports in Europe.

The Torre del Oro was once the southernmost of a series of protective towers punctuating Seville's Almohad-era town walls (see no. 37). Three more towers stand nearby, namely the octagonal Torre de la Plata (Tower of Silver) on Calle Santander, the Torre del Bronce (Tower of Bronze) in the former Royal Mint of Seville (Real Casa de la Moneda de Sevilla) on Calle Santander, and the Torre Abd-al Aziz at the corner of Calle Santo Tomás and Avenida de la Constitución.

The Torre del Oro may be one of Seville's oldest extant structures but there is a monument not far away that recalls even earlier events. On a busy roundabout several streets east is an equestrian statue of Rodrigo Díaz de Vivar (c.1043–1099), the Castilian knight known to the Moors as El Cid. He famously conquered Valencia in 1094 and for a while ruled an independent pluralistic society supported by Christians and Moors alike.

Other locations nearby: 4, 23, 25, 55

25 Home of the Performing Arts

El Arenal, the Teatro de la Maestranza at Paseo de Cristóbal Colón 22 (note: tickets are sold from the box office in the adjacent Jardin de la Caridad)

As its name suggests, the neighbourhood of El Arenal was originally a sandy area on the banks of the Guadalquivir River. Located outside the city walls, it was in former times the ideal place for Seville's Royal Shipyard (Reales Atarazanas) and Arsenal (Real Maestranza). It was the demolition of the Arsenal that eventually created space for a very different structure.

The Teatro de la Maestranza at Paseo de Cristóbal Colón 22 was built as a cultural venue for Seville's Expo '92. As such it was designed to represent the modern face of Andalucia. The architects Aurelio del Pozo and Luis Marín opted for a sleek cylindrical structure, with little ornamentation beyond the red, white and blue stripes on the domed roof. As a concession to the past, access is by means of the old riverside frontage of the Arsenal, including its original 19th century ironwork.

The circular footprint of the building serves a dual purpose. Primarily it provides for a column-free interior so as not to obscure the audience's sight lines; a secondary consideration is that it echoes the circular form of the nearby Plaza de Toros bullring. Both the bullring and the Arsenal were founded as part of the Real Maestranza de Caballería, a noble academy established for cavalry training (see no. 26).

The interior of the building is particularly striking. The rows of neatly-upholstered wooden seats with room for 1,800 spectators rise in tiers from the stage to the back of the building. Above them a coffered wooden ceiling ensures excellent acoustics, as do the large sound-boards attached to the walls. The venue's first performance, an opera, took place in 1991 just prior to the inauguration of the Expo. This and subsequent performances quickly catapulted it, along with its resident Royal Seville Symphony Orchestra (Real Orquesta Sinfónica de Sevilla), into the cultural limelight.

Despite being mainly devoted to opera, the Teatro de la Maestranza also stages performances of *Zarzuela*, Spain's own brand of operetta, as well as theatrical performances, *flamenco* and other shows. Many international opera, theatre and dance companies visit Seville to perform at the venue. Unfortunately in 1992 tragedy struck during a rehearsal by the Opéra national de Paris of Verdi's *Otello*. A part of the scenery collapsed, killing a member of the chorus and injuring dozens more. The Madrid tenor Plácido Domingo, who was set to play the role of Otelo but was in Germany at the time, flew immediately to Seville and visited the injured in hospital. The performance was cancelled and a court hearing later found that the visiting technical director was at fault.

On a happier note, a recent study determined that Seville has provided inspiration for 153 operas. That's considerably more than the number claimed by the great operatic cities of Rome, Venice and Paris put together. Among the most popular are Gioachino Rossini's *Il barbiere di Siviglia*, based on a French comedy by Pierre Beaumarchais (1732–1799), and Georges Bizet's *Carmen* (see nos. 7, 54). Others include Verdi's *La Forza del destino*, Beet-

A statue of the composer Mozart outside the Teatro de la Maestranza

hoven's *Fidelio*, Donizetti's *La Favorite*, and Mozart's *Le nozze di Figaro* and *Don Giovanni*, the latter derived from the great Sevillian literary myth of Don Juan (see no. 8).

A rather different-looking performance venue was erected for Seville's Ibero-American Exposition of 1929 (Exposición iberoamericana de 1929). The Teatro Lope de Vega in Parque de María Luisa was designed by Vicente Traver (1888–1966) in neo-Baroque style.

Other locations nearby: 2, 4, 22, 23, 24, 26

26   Death in the Afternoon

El Arenal, the Plaza de Toros de la Maestranza at Paseo de Cristóbal Colón 12 (note: bullfights staged intermittently on Sunday evenings between Easter and October, guided tours daily)

Poet Federico García Lorca (1898–1936) described bullfighting *(toreo)* as an "authentic religious drama". Certainly for a devotee there is nothing more thrilling than the sight of a *matador* pitting his (or occasionally her) wits against a raging bull from the security of a ringside seat. Indeed, in Andalucia, where bullfighting was born, it is considered by many a cornerstone of their cultural heritage.

Seville's Plaza de Toros de la Maestranza is arguably the finest bullring in Spain. It finds its origin in the Real Maestranza de Caballería, an academy founded in 1670 by the Spanish Crown to provide young Sevillian nobles with traditional equestrian and military training. Located outside the city walls in El Arenal, the academy's activities included bullfighting, which led to the construction in 1730 of Seville's first bullring.

The original structure was not ring-shaped at all but rectangular, where bullfighting on foot and horse was practised. This was replaced in 1761 with the current structure, its oval footprint a result of taking full advantage of the irregular plot of land available. Completed in 1881, the bullring retains its attractive neo-Baroque plastered façade in white and ochre, set off with blood red wooden doors.

Beyond these doors the bullring follows a plan based on Roman amphitheatres, where spectator blood sports originated. The audience sits in tiered stalls *(tendidos)* or in the balcony *(palcos)*, which incorporates the president's box *(presidencia)*. Opposite the box is the *Puerta de Cuadrillas* through which the matador enters, and the *Arrastre de Toros* through which the bulls are released. A protective barrier *(barreras)* separates the audience from the sand-covered arena, with wooden shields *(burladeros)* attached ringside for added protection. At a well-attended bullfight *(corrida)* up to 12,500 spectators are accommodated.

Bullfights in Seville are staged intermittently between Easter and October on Sunday evenings and have long been associated with the famous Seville Fair (Feria de Sevilla) (see no. 48). Each fight consists of three stages or *tercios*. In the first, the *Tercio de Varas*, the flamboyantly-dressed *matador* assesses the intelligence and speed of the bull by taunting it with his red cape *(capote)*. His assistants *(peones)* then draw the bull away towards horsemen *(picadores)*, whose job it is to weaken the animal's neck muscles using steel-tipped lances *(varas)*. During the second stage, the *Tercio de Bandilleras*, the wounded bull is further assessed and weakened by the *matador* by sticking pairs of darts *(bandilleras)* in its back. Finally, during the *Tercio de Muerte*, the *matador* makes a series of graceful passes at the bull with a smaller cape on a wooden pole *(muleta)*. He then picks his moment to dispatch the bull with a long thin sword, giving it a quick and clean death *(muerte)*.

A matador memorialised outside the Plaza de Toros de la Maestranza

Much controversy surrounds bullfighting today. Even Ernest Hemingway (1899–1961), an aficionado of the sport and author of *Death in the Afternoon*, predicted that "anything capable of arousing passion in its favour will surely raise as much passion against it". Those against will rightly stay well away but the curious might take a guided tour if only to see where the bouts take place. Included is the chapel, where matadors pray beforehand to the Virgin of Macarena, the first aid room *(enfermería)*, where injured matadors are treated, and a museum containing the head of the bull Islera, which fatally gored superstar *matador* Manolete (1917–1947) in Linares, Jaén. The bulls' heads hanging on the wall are often missing an ear, which is traditionally cut off and given to a victorious *matador*.

Fans of *Game of Thrones* will recognise the bullring as the Great Pit of Daznak in the Slaver's Bay city of Meereen, where a spectacular fight scene takes place featuring nobles, slaves and Khaleesi's dragon.

Other locations nearby: 20, 21, 22, 23, 25

27 A Railway Station Reinvented

El Arenal, the Plaza de Armas Shopping Centre (Centro Comercial Plaza de Armas) on Plaza la Légion

Seville's most unusual shopping centre is surely the Plaza de Armas Shopping Centre (Centro Comercial Plaza de Armas). Facing onto Plaza la Légion (El Arenal), it features a glorious Moorish revival façade behind which rises a colossal but unnecessary iron-and-glass roof. This architectural anomaly is explained not by aesthetics but by the fact that the building was originally a railway station.

Located on the banks of the Guadalquivir River, the Plaza de Armas Railway Station (Estación de Sevilla–Plaza de Armas) was inaugurated in 1859 by the Córdoba Railroad Company (Compañía del Ferrocarril de Córdoba). In those days though it was only a modest structure, where passengers boarded trains heading north only, hence its popular name, Estación de Córdoba (the San Bernardo Railway Station (Estación de San Bernardo) in Nervión, known as Estación de Cádiz, served southbound trains).

Within a few years the Córdoba-Seville line was integrated into the MZA Railroad Company (Compañia de los ferrocarriles Madrid–Zaragoza–Alicante) and it was they who in 1889 suggested enlarging the station into the building seen today. Completed in 1901 to a design by company engineers, it comprised two main elements. The first, facing onto the plaza, is the neo-Moorish entrance building, which would originally have contained a ticket office and waiting rooms. It is a fine example of the neo-*Mudéjar* style, which revived earlier Christian Moorish forms for the late-19th and 20th centuries (see no. 20). The horseshoe-shaped arches and ornate brickwork are informed by the Courtyard of the Lions at the Alhambra in Granada.

The second element is the train shed, with its soaring iron-and-glass roof. It is representative of the Sevillian Regionalist style (known also as *Andalucismo*), which deployed contemporary materials and construction techniques. The roof served not only to keep rain off waiting passengers but also to admit the maximum amount of light in an age of smoky, coal-fired locomotives.

Up until the time of the Spanish Civil War (1936–1939), the station was administered by the Andalusian Railways Company (Compañía de los Ferrocarriles Andaluces). Thereafter it came under the auspices of the National Network of Spanish Railways (Red Nacional de los Ferrocarriles Españoles), which drew up plans to reorganise Seville's

Neo-Mudéjar decoration at the old Plaza de Armas Railway Station

rail network. Taking Seville's Expo '92 as their cue, and the citywide urban renewal that came with it, they closed the Plaza de Armas Railway Station on 29th September 1990. For the next seven months all trains coming into Seville arrived instead at the San Bernardo Railway Station. This was then also closed and both stations replaced by the sleek new Seville Station–Santa Justa (Estación de Sevilla–Santa Justa) on Avenida de Kansas City. Since then, all of the city's rail traffic has passed that way.

Initially the abandoned Plaza de Armas Railway Station served as an Expo '92 pavilion, while the former martialling yard alongside it was turned into a car park and bus station. Only later, in 1999, was the old station reworked as a shopping and leisure centre. Thankfully the necessary remodelling left the basic structure intact and one can still imagine the trains and travellers that once frequented the place. The only real difference is that the far end of the train shed, which was once open to the elements, has now been closed off a new steel-and-glass window. Following suit, the old San Bernardo Railway Station has now also been refurbished as a shopping centre.

Other locations nearby: 28

28 Artists of the Golden Age

El Arenal, the Museum of Fine Arts (Museo de Bellas Artes) at Plaza del Museo 9

There are two main reasons behind Seville's passion for religious art. The Reconquest of Spain in 1492 reaffirmed the country's Christian faith and that same year Columbus set sail for the Americas. New World riches facilitated an economic boom, which then blossomed during the 17th century in a Golden Age of Baroque art. Spain's staunchly Catholic monarchy ensured that much of it was religious in theme.

The art of Seville's Golden Age is best represented by the holdings of the Museum of Fine Arts (Museo de Bellas Artes) at Plaza del Museo 9 (El Arenal). They are housed inside a former 17th century convent that was shuttered in 1835 during the liberal government's ecclesiastical confiscations *(la Desamortización)*. Secular fanatics took the opportunity to loot the building of its artistic treasures but fortunately enough was saved to form the basis of the museum. Private donations and public acquisitions have since bolstered the collection so that today it is second only to the Prado in Madrid.

The museum contains mainly Spanish works from the medieval period onwards. Chief among them are works by three great Golden Age artists, who together represent the painterly achievements of the so-called Seville School: Diego Velázquez (1599–1660), Francisco de Zurbarán (1598–1664) and Bartolomé Esteban Murillo (1617–1682).

Born into minor nobility in Seville, Velázquez was the least 'religious' artist of the three. As a court painter to King Philip IV (1605–1665) there was high demand for his portraits of statesmen, aristocrats and clergymen. They demonstrate an unusually fluid brushstroke for the time and a talent for expressing emotion through stark artistic realism, as seen in his *Retrato de D. Cristóbal Suárez de Ribera* (1620) (Room IV). With his landscapes, Velázquez was one of the first European artists to experiment with outdoor lighting.

By comparison, Zurbarán, who arrived in Seville as a teenager to take up an artistic vocation, fused realism with mysticism, as well as an emotional element pioneered by El Greco (1541–1614). The result was a style that chimed perfectly with Spain's spiritual climate at a time when the Catholic Church was waging war with Protestantism. To onlookers of the time, his works presented the miraculous in a believable and down-to-earth way. Typical is his *La Virgen de las Cuevas* (1655), which depicts the Virgin Mary protecting a group of Carthusian

La Virgen de las Cuevas (1655) by Francisco de Zurbarán

monks beneath her red cloak (Room X). Seville's Carthusian monks were great patrons of Golden Age art (see no. 42).

Another artist inspired by Velázquez was Seville-born Murillo. He superceded Zurbarán's strict realism with a preference for warm colours and soft light. This created an even more accessible style that found favour throughout the Catholic world. His favourite subject was the Virgin Mary and he depicted her in dozens of works on the theme of the Immaculate Conception. A fine example is his *Inmaculada Concepción la Niña* (1678) showing a wistful Virgin draped with a blue shawl surrounded by a cloud of chubby cherubs (Room V).

Of course, the Museum of Fine Arts contains works by a host of other similarly talented Baroque and Renaissance artists. Notably these include the painter Juan de Valdés Leal (1622–1690), his famously sombre and dramatic works given an entire room (Room VIII).

Murillo is the only Golden Age artist to warrant his own museum in Seville. The Casa de Murillo is housed in the painter's birthplace at Calle Santa Teresa 8 (Santa Cruz) not far from the lovely gardens that also bear his name (Jardines de Murillo).

Other locations nearby: 27

29 The Largest Wooden Structure

La Macarena, the Metropol Parasol in the Plaza de la Encarnación

Straddling the boundary between Santa Cruz and La Macarena is a wooden wonder. The Metropol Parasol in the Plaza de la Encarnación is a public sculpture, multipurpose leisure venue and viewing platform all rolled into one. It also lays claim to being the world's largest wooden structure.

The idea for the structure, which was unveiled in 2011, can be traced back to 1973. It was then that Seville's first market hall, which had stood in the plaza since 1842, was demolished due to structural failings. The site then lay empty until 2003, when the City Council announced a competition to build something new.

The winner of the competition was German architect Jürgen Mayer (b. 1965), who came up with something unexpected, at least it was back in 2003, when Mayer's distinctive spatial *œuvre* was unknown. Since then his penchant for bold organic forms exploring the relationship between nature and technology has been manifested in remarkable public buildings in Germany, Denmark and Georgia.

In Seville, Mayer sought inspiration from the man-made Gothic vaulting of Seville Cathedral (Catedral de Sevilla) and the naturally-twisted Strangler fig trees in the Plaza del Cristo de Burgos (Santa Cruz). He then set about designing six enormous parasol-shaped structures covering an area of 490 by 230 feet and supported on six sturdy concrete columns. The parasols were constructed using 3,500 pieces of Finnish pine held together by 16 million screws and nails. The result, when seen from a distance, is of a grove of giant mushrooms hence the structure's nickname *Las Setas de Sevilla* (The Mushrooms of Seville).

In practical terms the structure's function is two-fold. Firstly, it is a public amenity, one that locals have grown to love despite the project initially provoking anger among those who favoured something more conservative. Up inside the central parasols there is a restaurant, as well as space for private events. Beneath the parasols there is a large shaded square covering almost 40,000 square feet, where public gatherings, performances and displays take place. At ground level there is the current incarnation of the old market, the Mercado de la Encarnación, with around 40 stalls and catering stands. And in the basement

The Metropol Parasol fills the Plaza de la Encarnación

there is the Antiquarium, a museum in which historic artefacts recovered during the construction work are displayed, including Roman and Moorish remains.

The structure's other practical function is as a viewpoint. Two of the six concrete columns contain elevators that whisk visitors up to a serpentine panoramic walkway running 800 feet along the rim of the parasols. Beginning at a height of around 70 feet, the walkway rises to just over over 90 feet, all the while taking in expansive views not only of the wooden construction but also of the surrounding cityscape.

The Plaza de la Encarnación in which the Metropol parasol stands is named for an Augustinian convent built in 1591 and destroyed by Napoleonic troops in 1810. Before that the area was occupied by nobles following the Reconquest of Seville by King Ferdinand III of Castile (1201–1252). Remarkably the Guadalquivir River once ran near here and during Roman times the area formed part of the busy port of Hispalis.

After leaving the Metropol Parasol take a look inside the nearby Iglesia de la Anunciación on Calle Laraña. One of Seville's finest Renaissance buildings, it contains a crypt in which several illustrious Sevillians are laid to rest. The Hermandad del Valle, one of Seville's famous lay brotherhoods, is based in this church (see no. 38).

Other locations nearby: 17, 18, 32, 33

30 The Columns of Hercules

La Macarena, the Plaza de la Alameda de Hércules

Something curious is behind railings on Calle Mármoles (Santa Cruz). Three Egyptian granite columns stand alone, their presence at odds with the surrounding buildings. A clue to their original purpose is in the street name: Street of the Marbles. The marbles in question once formed part of the colonnade of a Roman temple or public building from the time of Emperor Hadrian (76 BC–138 AD). They are regarded as Seville's oldest standing structure.

The Romans arrived in Spain in 206 BC after achieving a decisive victory over the Carthaginians. Realising the wealth of the Iberian Peninsula, Roman General Scipio Africanus (236–183 BC) settled a contingent of veteran troops on a hill some six miles north-west of what is now Seville. Called Itálica, it was the first Roman city founded outside Italian territory, and is where Emperor Hadrian was born.

The Romans set about dividing the land they called Hispania into provinces. Itálica found itself in Baetica, where it grew into a typical residential Roman city. Never subsequently built over, Itálica's well-preserved ruins include villas, public baths and a magnificent amphitheatre. The city, however, did not exist in isolation. Nearby on the banks of the Guadalquivir River a commercial colony was developed out of a former Phoenician trading settlement called Hisbaal. Renamed Hispalis (or more formally Colonia Iulia Romula), it exported olive oil and wheat to Rome and became one of the region's great commercial centres.

Hispalis would eventually morph into Seville but today there are few visible Roman remains beyond the columns on Calle Mármoles. Fortunately, archaeologists have been able to fill in some of the gaps. We now know, for example, that frequent flooding of the Guadalquivir necessitated that the sandy banks of Hispalis were consolidated with wooden pilings. Remains of these have been unearthed along Calle Sierpes and in the Plaza de San Francisco.

The pilings illustrate the course of the Guadalquivir in Roman times, which extended northwards through what is now an elongated plaza called Alameda de Hércules (La Macarena). White poplars (álamos in Spanish) and café-bars now line the river's former course. At the southern end is a pair of Roman columns removed in 1574 from the building on Calle Mármoles. They support statues of Hercules, Seville's mythical founder, and Julius Caesar (100–44 BC), who served as a provincial official *(quaestor)* in Baetica before becoming emperor. It was Caesar who commissioned a protective stone wall around Hispalis (replacing an earlier Cathaginian timber stockade), as well as an aqueduct bringing potable water from the east (see nos. 14, 37).

Various important streets and key buildings have also been surmised. Today's Plaza de la Alfalfa, for example, was probably the crossroads of Hispalis's two main streets: the north–south Cardo Maximus and the east–west Decumanus Maximus. Here would have stood the Roman Forum, with its temples, baths and markets (a Roman-era cistern has been revealed beneath Plaza de la Pescadería). A basilica and curia probably stood near Plaza del Salvador. Without excavations, however, the rest is pure guesswork. Some tantalising small finds from Roman Seville are displayed in the city's Archaeological Museum (Museo Arqueológico)

Roman columns mark the start of the Plaza de la Alameda de Hércules

at Plaza América 51 (Parque de María Luisa) although currently the more impressive material is from Itálica (see no. 50).

The arrival of the Visigoths in 415 was the beginning of the end for Roman Spain – and the start of another chapter in the long history of Seville.

Other locations nearby: 31

31 Seville's Oldest Markets

La Macarena, the Historic Thursday Market (Mercadillo Historico del Jueves) and the Mercado de Feria on Calle Feria

Seville's northern neighbourhood of La Macarena is devout, working-class and still somewhat off tourist track. It's the place to see regular Sevillians at work, play and prayer, and there is nowhere better than Calle Feria. The area's main shopping street, it is lined with churches, shops and bars, and two of the city's oldest markets.

Stretching northwards a half mile from Calle Madre María de la Purísima to Calle Resolano, Calle Feria offers numerous inviting addresses. They include Antigüedaded El Pianillo at number 15, a remarkable antiques shop bursting with religious art, old books and painted tiles salvaged from nearby convents. Casa Vizcaíno at number 27 is a good place to pause for a glass of sherry or beer, and to appreciate how easily in Seville the secular can sit alongside the sacred. A little farther along, Dado at number 37 provides religious paraphernalia for feast days and Holy Week (Semana Santa), whilst next door is Jueves, a vintage clothing store selling everything from top hats to Hawaiian shirts.

This same stretch of Calle Feria is also the setting for the weekly Historic Thursday Market (Mercadillo Historico del Jueves). Seville's oldest market, it is documented as far back as the 13th century, when it is thought all manner of goods were traded here. Today it is very much a fleamarket, where old cameras, secondhand *flamenco* dresses and even replacement hands for effigies of the Virgin can be purchased. As with all fleamarkets it is advisable to arrive early to snap up the bargains.

Where Calle Feria crosses Calle Peris Mencheta stands the 13th century Iglesia de Omnium Sanctorum, one of Seville's oldest churches and a fine example of Gothic–*Mudéjar* (Christian Moorish) architecture, with a fine minaret-style bell tower. Alongside it is the Mercado de Feria, a market hall built in 1862 to a design by municipal architect Balbino Marrón y Ranero (1812–1867). A market has operated here since the 18th century and it remains as popular as ever, especially in the morning when the various stalls are laid out with fresh local produce. These include butchers (carnicería), fishmongers (pescadería), greengrocers (verdulería), fruiterers (frutería), brewers (cervecería), ice cream and cake manufacturers (heladería y pastelería), herbalists (herboristería) and florists (floristería). At the back of the hall is the Lonja de Feria, a recently-opened 'gastro market' aimed at a younger

Carved hands for effigies of the Virgin at the Historic Thursday Market

audience, with a seafood *tapas* bar selling paella, oysters and soups, and live music at the end of the week.

Calle Feria runs out of steam farther north but not before passing an eye-catching ceramic wall advertisement for *Sandeman* sherry at number 117.

Seville has several other historic covered markets notably the triple-aisled Mercado del Arenal (1947) at Calle Pastor y Landero 4 designed by architect Juan Talavera y Heredia (1880–1960) and the Mercado de Triana (1823), which sits over the ruins of the medieval Castle of San Jorge, once the seat of the Spanish Inquisition (see no. 45). There is also the Charco de la Pava fleamarket on Avenida de Carlos III (Isla de Cartuja), which is held on Sundays, as is the collectors' fair in the Plaza del Cabildo (Santa Cruz) (see no. 22). Other street markets have fallen by the wayside notably the longstanding animal market on Plaza de Alfalfa (Santa Cruz), which having been established in 1852 (but with roots stretching back to Moorish times) was abandoned in 2005 at the height of the bird flu epidemic.

Other locations nearby: 30, 32, 36

32 The Palacio de las Dueñas

La Macarena, the Palacio de las Dueñas at Calle Dueñas 5

Much of the district of La Macarena was once surrounded by Seville's city wall. As a result, its streets are like those of neighbouring Santa Cruz, narrow and densely packed. Respite from the heat and bustle is provided by various leafy *plazas*, as well as the gardens of the enchanting Palacio de las Dueñas at Calle Dueñas 5.

The palace is named after the Monastery of Santa María de las Dueñas (from the Latin *Dominus* meaning Lord), which until the late-19th century stood opposite. Built in the late-15th century during Seville's economic boom, it was originally home to the Pineda family, Lords of Casabermeja near Málaga.

In 1496, the family was forced to sell up to raise ransom money to retrieve a family member imprisoned by the Moors. The new owner was noblewoman Catalina de Ribera (1447–1505), widow of the Governor of Andalucia, Pedro Enríquez de Quiñones (d. 1493). It was her descendants who shaped the palace into the building seen today. In 1612, it passed through marriage to the Dukes of Alba and it has remained their official residence ever since. In 2016, on the initiative of the 19th Duke, Carlos Fitz-James Stuart, the palace was opened to the public.

The palace is essentially Renaissance in style but like the contemporary Casa de Pilatos, it incorporates Gothic and *Mudéjar* (Christian Moorish) elements (see no. 15). Access is by means of a neo-Classical carriage entrance emblazoned with the Dukes of Alba's crest made with tiles *(azulejos)* from the ceramic workshops in Triana (see no. 47). This gives onto a leafy courtyard beyond which is the entrance *(apeadoro)* to the palace proper. At its heart is the *Patio Principal* or main courtyard, a typically Andalucian feature. Here it consists of a green space divided into four on the principle of traditional Islamic paradise gardens, with a fountain in the centre and surrounded by a two-storey *Mudéjar* arcade, with Gothic balustrades above.

Leading off the *patio* is a series of grand rooms containing art, antiques and ceramics accumulated by the Dukes of Alba, together with a selection of their letters and family photos. Highlights include *La creación de Eva* by the Florentine artist Francesco Furini (1600–1646) (famous for his sensual *sfumato* style), *Cristo coronado de espinas* by the Spanish Tenebrist painter José de Ribera (1591–1652), and a watercolour by Jackie Kennedy (1929–1994) painted during her stay in

1960. One room contains an interesting collection of artefacts pertaining to Seville's famous April Fair (Feria de Abril) (see no. 48).

The finest room is undoubtedly the Salón de Gitana (Gypsy Hall) reached through an ornately carved *Plateresque* archway. Presided over by a sculpture of a *flamenco* dancer by Mariano Benlliure (1862–1947), it contains a fine collection of Flemish tapestries.

Despite being hemmed in by surrounding buildings, the palace gardens are beautiful. Lemon trees and towering palms transport the visitor far from the dusty city outside, and the Bougainvillea covering the palace façade is glorious when in bloom. The Spanish poet Antonio Machado (1875–1939), who was born here, extolled such beauty in his verse.

The delightful main courtyard at the Palacio de las Dueñas

Don't miss the family chapel added in the 16th century. Like its counterpart at the Casa de Pilatos, it has a glazed tile dado and a Gothic rib-vaulted ceiling. Over the altar hangs a painting of Saint Catalina of Sienna by Florentine artist Neri di Bicci (1419–1491). The explorer Amerigo Vespucci (1454–1512) is said to have married here after settling in Seville in the early-16th century.

Other locations nearby: 31, 33, 36

33 Where Tapas Were Invented

La Macarena, the El Rinconcillo tapas bar at Calle Gerona 40

There are few better backdrops against which to observe Andalucian life than a *tapas* bar. In Spanish cities and villages alike, it is where locals gather to eat, drink and make merry. A regional institution dating back to the 19th century, the *tapas* bar has today found favour around the world.

The name *tapas* derives from the tasty bites served as accompaniments to drinks around 1pm and again from around 8pm onwards. Their use originated in the 19th century, when bartenders covered a customer's glass with a saucer *(tapa)* to keep flies away. In time, the saucer was accompanied by a slice of Manchego cheese *(Queso manchego)* or a strip of dry-cured Iberian ham *(Jamón Ibérico)* or a handful of olives *(aceitunas)* – and so the *tapas* bar was born.

Remarkably, the bar where *tapas* are said to have been invented still survives in Seville (and if it wasn't here then this *tapas* bar is

Dry-cured Iberian
hams hanging at the
El Rinconcillo tapas bar

still Seville's oldest). El Rinconcillo at Calle Gerona 40 (La Macarena) opened its doors as a simple tavern back in 1670. The current owners, the De Rueda family, acquired the property in 1858. In 1897 they acquired the neighbouring house at Calle Alhondiga 2, which until the 1960s served as a grocer's store (*abacería*), thereby creating the L-shaped premises seen today (see no. 21).

The proprietors of El Rinconcillo have gone to great lengths to retain their property's traditional character. Original features include geometric wall ceramics (*azulejos*) made in Triana, ornate wooden shelves lined with dusty bottles, floor tiles from Tarifa, and cured hams suspended from the wooden ceiling. Customers' bills are still chalked on the mahogany bar and only wiped off when settled. As with other *tapas* bars, El Rinconcillo has its specialities, including *croquetas* (potato croquettes filled with ham or cod), *tortilla española* (potato and onion omelette) and *solomillo ibérico* (Iberian tenderloin).

While most tapas bars offer a dozen or so *tapas* there are well over 50 documented – from simple cured meats, salted nuts and cheeses to more elaborate cooked dishes. These might include *Albóndigas* (meatballs in spicy tomato sauce), *Berenjenas rellenas* (stuffed aubergine), *Lomo al Jerez* (pork loin in sherry sauce), *Rabo de toro* (bull's tail) and *Costillas al miel* (honey-baked spare ribs). Pescatarians will be pleased to find small fish on the menu dusted in flour then fried in olive oil (*Pescaito frito*). It's worth remembering a full portion of *tapas* is called a *ración*.

Tapas are traditionally accompanied by a glass of chilled *fino*, the driest of Spain's five types of sherry and the preferred type in Andalucia. It was the Phoenicians who introduced the vine to Spain's Jerez region almost 3,000 years ago whence the word 'sherry' is derived. However, it was British merchants during the 15th century who made the most of the region's chalky soil and grape varieties by fortifying local wines with grape spirit to produce sherry.

Tapas bar-hopping (*tapeo*) is popular in Seville. Not far from El Rinconcillo is Eslava at Calle Eslava 3, where reinvented *tapas* include an award-winning slow-cooked egg in caramelised sauce. The defiantly old-fashioned Bar Casa Plácido at Calle Mesón del Moro 5 (Santa Cruz) offers *Huevos a la flemenca* (baked eggs with spicy tomatoes), whilst the family-run Bodeguita Casablanca at Calle Adolfo Rodriguez Jurado 12 (El Arenal) provides good fish and seafood *tapas*. As an aside, lovers of street art should visit Lobo López at Calle Rosario 15 (El Arena) for its etched mural by Portuguese street artist Vhils (b. 1987).

Other locations nearby: 16, 29, 32

34 Ora et Labora

La Macarena, a tour of convents and churches including the Convento de Santa Paula at Calle Santa Paula 11 (note: only ring doorbell during opening hours)

You know you're crossing into Seville's most devout district when you peek into the 18th century Iglesia de San Antonio Abad at Calle Alfonso XII 3 (Santa Cruz). Home to Seville's Brotherhood of Silence (Hermandad del Silencio), its forecourt is a sea of flickering red candles placed there by parishioners and penitents alike.

Across the road is La Macarena, a staunchly Catholic working-class district. Encompassing several neighbourhoods named for saints, it boasts a dozen or so well-attended parish churches and almost as many convents. Several of them can be explored by heading east to Plaza San Pedro and its namesake 14th century Iglesia de San Pedro. One of the area's many Gothic–Mudéjar (Christian Moorish) churches – note the tower's Moorish-style polylobed windows – it was later given a Baroque belfry and portal. Behind the church on Calle Doña Maria Coronel is the contemporary Convento de Santa Inés. Despite being a cloistered (closed) community, the Poor Clare nuns here sell their homemade sweets (yemas) to outsiders via a discreet revolving drum (torno) in the courtyard.

Next stop is the Iglesia de Santa Catalina on Calle Alhondinga. Another 14th century Gothic–Mudéjar edifice, it occupies the former site of a mosque (see no. 9). Inside are chapels with statues by Baroque sculptor Pedro Roldán (1624–1699). Two more Gothic–Mudéjar churches, the Iglesia de San Román and the Iglesia de San Marcos, overlook eponymous plazas several streets north, the latter with a nave incorporating unique Moorish-style horseshoe arches.

The Iglesia de San Marcos is surrounded by no less than three convents. The Convento de Santa Isabel was founded in 1490 and is occupied by the Philippine Daughters, whilst the 16th century Convento de Santa María del Socorro houses the Order of the Immaculate Conception. Most interesting is the partially-cloistered Convento de Santa Paula at Calle Santa Paula 11. Established in the 15th century, it is home to some 30 nuns from around the world. Ring the doorbell at number 11 to visit the convent museum, with its superb Neapolitan cribs, and gain a glimpse of the nuns' secretive quarters. By request visitors will also be shown the window grilles *(locatorio)*, where the nuns receive visitors without being seen. In the peaceful courtyard there is a shop selling homemade orange marmalade and *yemas* reflecting the nuns' motto *Ora et Labora* (Prayer and Work).

More churches and convents can be explored nearer the river. Start with the Iglesia de San Vicente (yet another 14th century Gothic–*Mudéjar* church) at Calle Miguel Cid 1. A couple of streets away at Calle Cardenal Spínola 8 is the Convento de Santa Rosalia founded in 1700 for the Capuchin Poor Clares and containing a superb collection of Baroque altarpieces. Farther north on the same street is the Iglesia de San Lorenzo (again Gothic–*Mudéjar*) and the conjoined Basílica

Orange marmalade made by the sisters at the Convento de Santa Paula

de Jesús del Gran Poder. Like most Sevillian churches, both double as headquarters for lay brotherhoods (variously called *hermanadades* or *cofradias*) that play an intrinsic part in the city's Holy Week (Semana Santa) (see no. 38).

Continuing north past the Convento de las Repadoras at Calle Santa Clara 12 (now used by the Ukrainian Greek Catholic Church) is the sprawling former Convento de Santa Clara (accessible from Calle Becas), which is now a cultural centre (Espacio Santa Clara). A Gothic tower in the garden, the Torre de Don Fadrique, is all that remains of a *Mudéjar* palace.

Finally, at the end of the street, is the Monasterio de San Clemente, which boasts a church with a breathtakingly intricate *Mudéjar* wooden ceiling *(artesonado)*.

Convents elsewhere also sell homemade sweets notably the 15th century Dominican Convento Madre de Dios at Calle San José 4 (Santa Cruz).

Other locations nearby: 35, 36, 37

35 The Corralónes Art Collectives

La Macarena, a tour of art collectives beginning with the Corralón de Pelicano at Plaza Pelícano 4 (note: be aware that most artisans do not work fixed hours and may not always be on site)

Since Moorish times, traditional family life in Seville has played out in shady, private courtyards away from the street. This same principle has also been applied to working life in the form of *corralónes*, courtyards surrounded by workshops and studios. Commonplace during the 19th century, most were abandoned as manufacturing processes developed. The few that have survived are now being reoccupied by a new generation of artisans, notably in the working-class district of La Macarena.

Corralónes are perfectly suited to today's art collectives wherein independent craftspeople ply their trades: from painters, potters, blacksmiths and sculptors to musicians, poets, filmmakers and *flamenco* dancers. The collective concept gives these people not only an inspiring environment in which to work but also the freedom to work alone or together. Visiting these oases of creativity makes for an engaging thematic tour, well away from the tourist hotspots of Santa Cruz.

This tour begins with the Corralón de Pelicano at Plaza Pelícano 4. Charming as it is, with its quaint cobblestones, pots of flowers and peach tree, it's what goes on behind the unassuming garage-style doors that matters. This was one of Seville's first industrial estates and it still retains a novel vibe thanks to its colourful roster of around fifty artisans. This currently includes a woodworker, sculptor, *flamenco* dancer and African drummer. An enduring co-working arrangement is enjoyed by potter Juan Monje and guitar luthier César Hashmi, who occupy different floors of a studio just inside the main gate. Their neighbours include a small number of non-artists who have idiosyncratic homes here, clearly keen to soak up the creative atmosphere.

Around the corner from Plaza Pelícano is the Pasaje Mallol. Here again a variety of creative endeavours are being pursued with passion, this time along an entire street. The workspaces include an artist's studio pulsating with colour and a metalworker's shop where sparks fly. In common with the Plaza Pelícano, the artisans are keen to engage with an interested public. This is especially apparent during their shared open days to which people of all ages are welcome. Children

Potter Juan Monje and luthier César Hashmi at the Corralón de Pelicano

will always find something to excite them, and the proceedings are helped along with live music and street performers.

A couple of streets farther west at Calle San Luis 70 is Rompemoldes. The art collective here represents a new twist on the traditional *corralóne* being housed in a sleek new-build structure that would sit well in Barcelona or Berlin. The mindset remains the same though, with operatives less interested in creating works for exhibition or well-to-do clients and more concerned about creating affordable work all year round and on their own terms. This honest working approach links today's *corralónes* directly to their historic antecedents in a manner typical for Seville. The twenty five studios include a ceramicist, bookbinder, jeweller and fashion designer.

Operated in a similar vein to a *corralóne* is La SinMiedo at Avenida la Cruz Roja 62. This café and cultural centre, with its feminist ethos, was originally a coal yard (carbonería). Today its Isadora Duncan Room hosts a variety of exhibitions, poetry recitals, concerts and dance performances.

Though not classed as a *corralóne* (since there is no manufacturing on the premises), the Mercado de Artesania de Sevilla El Postigo at Calle Arfe 29 (El Arenal) should be mentioned here. Open since 1980, this former post office building contains a dozen or more stalls selling jewellery, leatherwork and ceramics all made by local craftspeople. The building is worth a look for its Escher-like double staircase.

Other locations nearby: 34, 36, 37

36 A Spanish Baroque Masterclass

La Macarena, the Iglesia de San Luis de los Franceses at Calle San Luis 37

Seville in the 17th century experienced both wealth from trade with the Americas alongside plague and poverty. This combination created a surge of religious fervour made tangible through the artistic style known as Baroque. Deployed extensively in churches, it is defined by sweeping curves, lofty cupolas and a riot of stucco, gilt and painted decoration. For churchgoers, such a novel theatrical style represented the triumph of Catholicism over adversity.

Baroque first appeared in Italy during the early-17th century and gradually spread across Europe (the name is derived from the Portuguese for 'rough pearl' in deference to Baroque's penchant for encrusted ornament). Instrumental in the spread was the Society of Jesus, which arrived in Seville in 1554. A bastion of the Spanish Counter Reformation, these Jesuits initially erected the Renaissance-style Iglesia de la Anunciación at Calle Laraña 1 (Santa Cruz). This was later superceded by Seville's finest Baroque church, the Iglesia de San Luis de los Franceses at Calle San Luis 37.

Constructed between 1699 and 1730, and a masterclass in Spanish Baroque, this church was built to a design by architect Leonardo de Figueroa (1654–1730). The dedication to Saint Louis, the medieval French monarch and brother of King Ferdinand III (1201–1252), who wrested Seville from the Moors, was made at the behest of the noblewoman who donated the land. It also reflects the Jesuits' desire to forge a good relationship with Spain's new Bourbon (French) kings so as to avoid expulsion.

The front of the church is red brick, with decorative stone pilasters, book-ended by two octagonal towers. Although it is not obvious, it forms one end of a Greek cross over the centre of which is placed a cupola. Seen from inside, this is a truly magnificent feature seemingly supported by sixteen spiral columns (although in reality the work is done by four cleverly disguised stone pillars). The wall paintings in the cupola surrounding the word *Religio* are by Lucas de Valdés Carasquilla (1661–1725) and incorporate Biblical motifs, including the Ark of the Covenant and a menorah. The paintings over the main entrance depict Saint Ignatius of Loyola, who founded the Jesuits in 1540.

The painted cupola at the Iglesia de San Luis de los Franceses

The church contains much symbolism for the eagle-eyed. Look out for the eight-pointed star at the cupola's apex representing the Eight Beatitudes, the Fleur-de-Lys atop the columns used as a symbol of French royalty, and the convex Venetian mirrors in the side chapels recalling the Virgin Mary's motto on purity ('speculum sine macula').

Following their expulsion in 1767 by King Charles III (1716–1788), the Jesuits abandoned the church only to return later and be expelled again in 1835. Since then the building has served various purposes and today belongs to the Provincial Council of Seville.

Other noteworthy examples of Sevillian Baroque include the Iglesia del Salvador on Plaza del Salvador (Santa Cruz), with its incredible gilded altarpiece, the Iglesia de la Magdalena on Calle San Pablo (El Arenal), with its colourful belfries, the Capilla de San José on Calle Jovellanos (Santa Cruz), with its exuberantly decorated apse, and the Iglesia de Santa María la Blanca at Calle Santa María la Blanca 5 (Santa Cruz) (see no. 9).

An extraordinary secular Baroque building is the vast San Telmo Palace on Avenida de Roma (Parque de María Luisa). It is distinguished by a magnificently flamboyant portal in the ultra-Baroque *Churrigueresque* style and is again the work of Leonardo de Figueroa. Built originally as a naval college, it is today the headquarters of the Government of Andalucia (Junta de Andalucía).

Other locations nearby: 31, 32, 34, 35, 37, 38

37 Last of the City Walls

La Macarena, a walk along the Walls of Seville (Murallas de Sevilla) beginning at the Puerta de Córdoba on Calle Puerta de Córdoba

Beyond the fortified confines of the Real Alcázar, the casual visitor is hard pressed to find evidence for Seville's old city wall. Built long ago for defence and flood protection, and demolished during the 19th century, all that remains are a few gates, towers and stretches of curtain wall. It makes for an interesting walk to track them down and to imagine how fortified Seville once looked.

Seville's first wall dates from the Roman period, when Julius Caesar (100–44 BC) was provincial official *(quaestor)* of Hispania Ulterior (see no. 30). Built between 68 and 65 BC to protect the Roman port of Hispalis, it encompassed much of what is today the *barrio* Santa Cruz between Avenida de la Constitucion and Avenida Menéndez Pelayo. It then tapered northwards to just beyond the Metropol Parasol.

This same wall was maintained during the Visigothic and early Moorish periods. Razed by the Vikings in 844, it was then rebuilt by Seville's Umayyad rulers although nothing remains. Later, in 1023, Abad I (984–1042), founder of the Abbadid dynasty and first independent Muslim ruler of Seville, commissioned a new crenellated brick wall as protection against Christian forces. Encircling twice the area of the original wall and punctuated by gates and towers, it encompassed the Real Alcázar to the south, ran northwards following the curve of the Guadalquivir River to Calle Resolana (La Macarena), then returned south down what is today Ronda de Capucinos to Avenida Menéndez Pelayo. Of this second wall several 13th century Almohad-era fragments remain, notably the famous Torre del Oro (Tower of Gold) (see no. 24).

The final phase of wall construction occurred after King Ferdinand III (1201–1252) had wrested Seville from the Moors in 1248. The Castilian monarchy retained the Moorish wall but modified it to include eighteen large and small gates *(puertas* and *postigos* respectively) and a hundred or so defence towers. Many of these were named for the trades that frequented them or else the places outside Seville to which they led.

With sustained peace, the wall's military function gradually decreased and it served instead as a customs barrier. Only after Spain's Glorious Revolution (1868) was it decided to demolish the wall so as not to hinder the city's growth. Of the fragments that escaped destruction the best runs along the northern boundary of La Macarena. Known as the Walls of Seville (Murallas de Sevilla), it starts on Calle Puerta de Córdoba, where a gateway survives of the same name. Dating from the Almohad era, it is one of four remaining gates and is still angled in typical Moorish style to foil invaders (today it backs onto the 17th century Iglesia de San Hermenegildo). From here a quarter of a mile of intact curtain wall winds northwards, incorporating eight towers (seven square and the octagonal Torre Blanca) and several *postigos*. The wall terminates at a second gate, the colourfully rebuilt Puerta de la Macarena, which has 12th century Almoravid origins.

A part of the old walls of Seville in La Macarena

Several other wall fragments are worth finding. Clockwise they include a curtain wall with towers in the Jardines des Valles, the crenelated walls of the Real Alcázar and the Postigo del Alázar (see no. 7), three towers adjacent to the Torre del Oro (see no. 24), another gate called the Postigo del Aceite (see no. 23), and further fragments in the Plaza del Cabildo and at Calle San Laureano 3. The word 'aceite' by the way is one of many Arabic loan words found in Spanish.

Other locations nearby: 34, 35, 36, 38

38 Holy Week

La Macarena, Holy Week (Semana Santa) and the Basílica
de la Macarena on Plaza de la Esperanza Macarena
(note: up to a million people attend Holy Week celebrations
so be prepared for crowded streets and late nights)

Nothing better illustrates Andalucia's fervent Catholicism than its Holy Week (Semana Santa) celebrations. Staged in the days leading up to Easter, they involve elaborate street processions commemorating Christ's Passion, as well as ecstatic adoration of the Virgin Mary. That this spirited public event has remained unchanged in five centuries makes it very special indeed.

Holy Week in Seville is undoubtedly the most spectacular Easter celebration found in any Spanish city. At its heart is a series of daily processions formed by decorated floats known as *pasos*. Each carries a life-sized wooden effigy representing either a scene from the Mysteries of the Rosary or a depiction of the stoic yet grieving Virgin. The processions are organised by lay brotherhoods – known as *cofradias* or *hermanadades* – each of which is attached to a particular church. Dating back to the 13th century, when they acted as police forces, these voluntary organisations today serve as neighbourhood representatives. More than sixty brotherhoods take part, with up to three *pasos* in each of the six or more daily processions. Accompanied by mournful brass bands and spectators filling the streets, they haul their effigies slowly to the cathedral and back. Processions from Seville's suburban *barrios* can take up to fourteen hours to make the round journey!

Members of the brotherhoods, known as *nazarenos*, accompany their *paso* dressed in long robes and pointed hoods *(capirotes)*. Those carrying crosses are repenting their sins, their hoods designed so they can do so anonymously. Other members are barely seen at all since they are the ones carrying the heavy *pasos* aloft on their shoulders.

The greater part of the journey is known as the *Estación de penitencia* (Stations of Penance); the last short section common to each procession as it reaches the cathedral is known as the *Carrera Oficial* (Official Route). The processions take place from Palm Sunday right through to Easter Sunday morning. The climax of the week is undoubtedly the night of Holy Thursday, when the now-candlelit processions arrive at the cathedral in time for the dawn of Good Friday, a time known as *Madrugá*.

Seville's most famous Holy Week effigy is the Virgin of Hope of Macarena (Virgen de la Esperanza de Macarena). Her image can be seen across the city on wall ceramics, posters and ornaments. The original life-sized effigy, however, is displayed in the neo-Baroque Basílica de la Macarena on Plaza de la Esperanza Macarena. Thought to have been crafted in the 17th century by Baroque sculptor Pedro Roldán (1624–1699), she has articulated wooden arms and human hair, with glass tears that emphasise her painted expression, somewhere between sorrow and ecstasy. She is dressed in a richly embroided mantle, trimmed with lace and sprinkled with jewels. The word *Esperanza* (Hope) is emblazoned on her chest.

Nazarenos during Seville's Holy Week celebrations

Normally the Virgin stands above the main altar. Only during Holy Week is she brought down and placed on her personal silver *paso* decorated with white wax flowers and candles. Her appearance on the streets in the early hours of Good Friday provokes the most ardent reaction from devotees, who clap, throw flower petals and cry *Guapa!* (Beautiful!), while singers project 'arrows' of praise *(saetas)* from palm-bedecked balconies, and deep-fried pastries glazed in honey or cinnamon *(pestiños)* are eaten.

Full details of when and where each *paso* takes place are available in the run-up to Holy Week. The various effigies can be viewed the rest of the year in their respective parish churches. The Macarena Virgin's silver *paso* is parked in the treasury of the Basílica de la Macarena, alongside a golden *paso* reserved for an effigy of Christ.

The Virgin of Hope is also venerated in the Capilla de los Marineros (Sailors' Chapel) at Calle Pureza 57 (Triana), where another magnificent effigy of the Virgen de la Esperanza graces the altar. Before being acquired in 1940 by the Brotherhood of the Esperanza de Triana, the chapel served as a cabaret, cinema and warehouse!

Other locations nearby: 36, 37, 39

39 The Day of Andalucia

La Macarena, the Parliament of Andalucia (Parlamento de Andalucía) on Calle San Juan de Ribera (note: guided visits by appointment only mid-Sep to mid-Jun with passport shown on entry)

Seville Cathedral (Catedral de Sevilla) may well be the city's icon but when it comes to Andalucia it's the city's parliament building that counts. Located in La Macarena, just beyond the line of the old city walls, it is here that the autonomous community's legislature goes about its important day-to-day business.

The Parliament of Andalucia (Parlamento de Andalucía) was instituted in 1981 by the Andalusian Charter of Autonomy. Since then its 109 members (representing Andalucia's eight provincial constituencies) have been elected every four years and tasked with four tasks: to elect a President, to pass legislation pertaining to the region, to pass the region's Budget, and to regulate the action of the region's governmental administration and the various bodies answerable to it (including public universities and Chambers of Commerce).

The date on which Andalucians voted to become an autonomous Spanish community was February 28th 1980. This has subsequently become known as the Día de Andalucía (Day of Andalucia) and celebrated with considerable gusto. The flag of Andalucia will often be seen draped from balconies, with bunting echoing its green-and-white stripes. In the Málaga region schools close for a *Semana Cultural* (Cultural Week) during which children enjoy a traditional Andalucian breakfast of toast with olive oil and orange juice *(Desayuno Andaluz)* and sing the regional anthem, the *Himno de Andalucía*.

Since the Día de Andalucía in 1992, the Parliament of Andalucia has occupied a four-square historic building on Calle San Juan de Ribera. Chosen for its size and availability, the magnificent Renaissance structure had lain empty for twenty years after its original function as a hospital came to an end. It was the government that undertook the necessary work to convert the hospital into a parliament.

Prior to 1972, the building served as the Hospital de las Cinco Llagas (Hospital of the Five Holy Wounds). Founded in 1500 by the noblewoman Catalina de Ribera (1447–1505), it was originally located near her home, the Casa de Pilatos (see no. 15). Only later, in 1546, did her son Don Fadrique Enríquez de Ribera (1476–1539) leave a bequest so that the present building could be constructed. Designed by Mar-

Hercules, Seville's legendary founder, and the Parliament of Andalucia

tín de Gainza (d. 1556), who was also responsible for Seville's Town Hall (Ayuntamiento) and the Royal Chapel (Capilla Real) at Seville Cathedral, it was intended to be laid out around ten courtyards though only nine were completed of which eight survive today (see no. 19). Despite this it soon became Europe's largest hospital. In a remarkably long history, the first patients were admitted in 1613 and the last during the 1960s. Distinctive elements of the design include a Baroque central portal by Asensio de Maeda (1547–1607), who also worked on the cathedral. The hospital church in the central courtyard was rendered in the Spanish Renaissance style by Hernán Ruiz the Younger (c.1514–1569) and contains an altarpiece built by Diego López Bueno (c.1568–1632). It is here that the plenary sessions of the Parliament of Andalucia take place today.

The parliament gardens consist of low topiary hedges interspersed with ornamental fountains. Also here is a modernist sculpture by the Malagueño artist José López García-Sigai (b. 1959). Depicting Hercules, Seville's legendary founder, with two lions and columns, it originally adorned the Andalucia Pavilion (Pabellón de Andaluciá) at Seville's Expo '92 (see no. 44).

Other locations nearby: 37, 38

40 A City for the Dead

Seville's only municipal burial ground, the Cemetery of San Fernando (Cementerio de San Fernando), sprawls northwards from the Calle Huerta de la Fontanilla in the city's Distrito Norte (North District). Opened in 1852, it contains poets, painters, bull fighters and *flamenco* performers.

Until the 19th century, Seville's middle and upper classes were buried in church vaults, with poorer people relegated to parish graveyards. Located within the city walls, these repositories inevitably became overcrowded and in 1800 contributed to an epidemic that killed around 14,000 people. This prompted the establishment in 1828 of Seville's first extramural municipal cemetery at the Hermitage of San Sebastián (today Seville's Parque Prado de San Sebastián near the Plaza de España). It included wall niches for the well-to-do and a mass grave for the poor. By 1850, however, the sheer number of bodies and issues with groundwater saw the cemetery abandoned.

The Cemetery of San Fernando was created to overcome such problems. Most importantly its twenty eight hectares, divided into three main sections around a central axis, were located well away from the city centre and offered near limitless capacity. The cemetery was designed by Seville's municipal architect Balbino Marrón y Ranero (1812–1867). He allowed for most people to be buried in the ground, with a limited number of wall niches for outsiders and those without family. Whereas the poor continued to be buried in simple ditches, imposing mausoleums were erected for magnates and their families. Designed by Balbini and other notable architects, including Aníbal González (1876–1929), these structures are the cemetery's most eye-catching features.

The cemetery also includes public monuments. One of these raised in 1861 commemorates the fallen of the Hispano–Moroccan War (1859–60) and takes the form of a Lycian tomb. Another is a bronze crucifix by local sculptor Antonio Susillo (1855–1896). Erected in 1895, it stands on the first of two roundabouts punctuating the half-mile-long avenue that forms the cemetery's main axis. It is known locally as the *Cristo de las Mieles* because in 1907 honey was seen running miraculously from Christ's mouth (though most likely it was from a beehive lodged inside the hollow sculpture).

The tomb of matador Joselito at the Cemetery of San Fernando

Many of Seville's great and good have their resting place here. They include a handful of legendary matadors, including José Gómez Ortega ('Joselito') (1895–1920), whose fatal goring triggered not only national grief but also Seville's famous Virgin of Macarena to be dressed in black (see no. 38). His bronze monument by Valencian sculptor Mariano Benlliure (1862–1947) consists of a life-sized funeral cortege carrying aloft his open coffin. Other celebrities include Seville-born painter José Villegas Cordero (1844–1921), actress and *copla* singer Juanita Reina (1925–1999), Spanish-Cuban singer Antonio Machín (1903–1977) and *flamenco* guitarist and composer Niño Ricardo (1904–1972).

In 1936, a distinct area in the north-west corner of the cemetery was set aside for Muslims. Here around ninety volunteers from the Spanish Protectorate of Morocco, who fell during the Spanish Civil War, are buried. Elsewhere four mass graves contain 3,800 Left Wing Republicans and anarchists from the same conflict, whilst another area holds the remains of around sixty members of Seville's Jewish community.

Seville's other historic cemetery of note is the tiny Cementerio de los Ingleses, which was an Anglican burial ground for the British. Initiated by English merchant John Cunningham, it opened in 1854 alongside the Monastery of San Jerónimo on Calle Marruecos. Like the San Fernando Cemetery, it was designed by Balbino Marrón y Ranero, only this time in an English style, with neo-Gothic tombs set among shrubbery. It is today abandoned and overgrown.

Other locations nearby: 41

41 Bridging the Guadalquivir

Isla de la Cartuja, the Puente del Alamillo connecting the Norte district and the Isla de la Cartuja

Seville sits on a bend in the Guadalquivir River. Its name comes from the Arabic *al-wadi al-kabir* meaning 'the great river' and indeed it is Spain's only great navigable waterway. Flowing for 408 miles across the width of Andalucia, it rises high in the Sierra de Cazorla and disgorges into the Atlantic just above Cádiz. In Roman times it was possible to travel from the sea all the way up to Córdoba. These days only the fifty mile stretch to Seville is passable.

Seville's heyday as Spain's only inland port came during the 16th century, when the likes of Columbus, Magellan and Vespucci set out to explore – and exploit – the New World. Treasure fleets returned laden with precious metals, cocoa beans, spices and dyes, including cochineal and indigo. Spain's monopoly on trade between 1503 and 1680 made Seville Europe's greatest port.

Remarkably throughout this period only one bridge connected Seville with the island suburb of Triana on the opposite shore. This was the Puente de Barcas (Bridge of Boats), a pontoon commissioned in 1171 by the Almohad caliph Abu Yaqub Yusuf (1135–1184). Used to reach an Almohad-era fortress, necropolis and pottery kilns, as well as the region of Aljarafe beyond, it remained Seville's sole river crossing for almost seven centuries.

By the 1680s, the silting of the Guadalquivir saw Seville's port relocated southwards from the Arenal – today it sits at the southern tip of the Los Remedios district – and the city's role as a port diminished in favour of Cádiz. Flooding was a persistent problem, too, but this was not addressed until the 20th century, when the arm of the river separating Seville from Triana was blocked at its northern end so as to create a backwater called the Canal de Alfonso XIII. This allowed the main body of the river to pass harmlessly west of Triana and the Isla de la Cartuja (see no. 42).

Seville's first permanent bridge, the Puente de Isabelle II, only opened in 1852 by which time the river's capricious geomorphology was better understood. A fine example of 19th century Andalucian wrought iron architecture *(Arquitectura de hierro)*, the bridge is referred to by proud locals as the Puente de Triana.

The bridge was considered revolutionary for its time and the same applies to one of Seville's more recent bridges. The Puente del Alamillo

Santiago Calatrava's Puente del Alamillo bridges the Guadalquivir River

connecting the city's Norte district with the Isla de la Cartuja opened in 1992 as part of citywide improvements undertaken for Seville's Expo '92 (see no. 44). Designed by the renowned Spanish architect Santiago Calatrava (b. 1951), it is of the cantilever spar cable-stayed type. That is to say it consists of a single pylon set on one bank, tilted backwards so as to counterbalance a 655-foot span suspended on 13 cables. The original design (abandoned due to financial restrictions) proposed a similar arrangement on the opposite bank but in the end the single pylon design proved no less striking. There is an elevated walkway for pedestrians and a viewing platform at the top of the pylon accessible by means of an enclosed stairway.

Seen from afar, the Puente del Alamillo continues to represent the aspirations of modern Seville. In this it is partnered by the Puente de la Barqueta a little way downstream. One of a handful of other bridges constructed as part of Expo '92, it is formed by a steel cable-tensed arch supported by triangular frames at each end.

Other locations nearby: 40

42 Island of the Carthusians

Isla de la Cartuja, the Monastery of Santa María de las Cuevas (Monasterio de Santa Mariá de las Cuevas) at Calle Américo Vespucio 2

For a long time as the Guadalquivir River flowed past Seville its course split to form an island on which grew the district of Triana. Repeated flooding, however, necessitated that during the 20th century the arm nearest Seville was blocked upstream creating the Canal de Alfonso XIII. The other arm was then straightened to carry floodwaters harmlessly away. In the process the island (in reality now a peninsula) was elongated northwards. Known as the Isla de la Cartuja (Island of the Carthusians), it was here that Seville's Expo '92 was staged (see no. 44). The island's name, however, speaks of an earlier history.

The island is named after the Monastery of Santa María de las Cuevas. Legend holds that in Moorish times the area was pitted with small caves excavated by potters in search of clay. Following the capture of Seville by the Christians in 1248, an image of the Virgin was discovered in one of these caves prompting the dedication of a chapel to Santa María de las Cuevas (Saint Mary of the Caves). During the 15th century, the Archbishop of Seville founded a monastery on the site in the Gothic–*Mudéjar* style. Created initially for the Franciscans, it later served the cloistered Carthusians.

As well as its patronage of Golden Age art, the Carthusian monastery's great claim to fame is that explorer Christopher Columbus (1451–1506) lodged here while planning his expeditions to the New World. Although when he died his remains were initially held in Valladolid, they were soon relocated to the monastery at the request of his son, Diego (1479–1526), where they remained until 1542. They currently reside in Seville Cathedral (see no. 2).

In 1810 during the Napoleonic invasion, the monastery was sacked and turned into barracks. The Carthusians returned in 1812 only to leave for good in 1836 under the ecclesiastical confiscations *(la Desamortización)* of Prime Minister Juan Álvarez Mendizábal (1790–1853). This nationwide anti-clerical action freed up much under-utilised land for the enterprising middle classes. One person to benefit was the Englishman Charles Pickman Jones (1808–1883). In 1839, having learned the ceramics' trade from his half brother and father, he leased the disused monastery and established the La Cartuja de Sevilla–Pickman ceramics' factory. By utilising the latest manufacturing methods, as

The Carthusian monastery that became a ceramics' factory

well as those of the traditional pottery workers of nearby Triana, Pickman made the *La Cartuja de Sevilla* brand one of the most popular in Europe and Latin America. He garnered numerous trade awards, supplied the Royal House and was eventually made Marquis of Pickman. Production at the site only finished in 1984, with the factory's tall chimney and distinctive bottle-shaped kilns still extant.

After being declared a national monument, the former monastery-turned-factory became a tourist attraction during Seville's Expo '92, the theme of which was the Age of Discovery. Later, in 1997, the complex was turned over to the Andalusian Centre of Contemporary Art (Centro Andaluz de Arte Contemporáneo). Aimed at promoting international modern art in all its facets, it has a permanent collection, including the giant head and hand filling two of the monastery gatehouse windows by Jaén-born multidisciplinary artist Cristina Lucas (b. 1973), and offers a busy calendar of temporary exhibits (see back cover). Visitors can also explore the old monastery grounds, with their chapels (one of which contains the tombs of several sleeping but surprisingly lifelike knights), cloisters, gardens and orchards. Look out for the huge South American ombú tree said to have been planted by Columbus' other son, Fernando (1488–1539).

Other locations nearby: 43, 44

43 Andalucia's Tallest Tower

Isla de la Cartuja, the Seville Tower (Torre Sevilla) at Calle Gonzalo Jiménez Quesada 2

For almost 450 years, Seville's tallest structure was the Giralda, the minaret-turned-belfry at the city's cathedral (see no. 2). Soaring 342 feet into the air, it was completed in its present form in 1568. Only in 2015 was it eventually eclipsed by the ultra-modern Seville Tower (Torre Sevilla), an event that caused some consternation among the city's architectural purists.

Located at the southern edge of the Isla de la Cartuja, on what was formerly the city's Expo '92 site, the Seville Tower was the city's first skyscraper. It was designed by the Argentine architect César Pelli (1926–2019), hence it being nicknamed the Pelli Tower during its seven-year construction. Pelli at the time was famous for having designed some of the world's best known tall buildings, including the Petronas Towers in Kuala Lumpur and the World Financial Center (Brooklyn Place) in New York City.

Constructed on an elliptical footprint, the Seville Tower rises to a height of 592 feet. It comprises 40 storeys – 37 above ground and three below – which together offer an impressive 732,000 square feet of space. Whilst much of this is taken up with offices, the top 12 storeys form the 5-star Eurostars Torre Sevilla Hotel. Reached by several of the tower's eight lifts, the hotel offers guests some remarkable views across the surrounding city. Although the tower lays claim to being the tallest building in Andalucia, however, it only ranks eighth tallest in Spain. The accolade of the country's tallest building goes currently to the Torre de Cristal in Madrid, which soars far above the Seville Tower to a height of 817 feet.

Perhaps not surprisingly, the construction of the Seville Tower proved controversial. Some critics went so far as to ask UNESCO to consider putting the city's World Heritage Sites – the Cathedral, Alcázar and Archivo de Indias – on their threatened list because of the tower's negative visual impact on the Old Town's skyline. UNESCO responded by asking for the tower's height to be reduced but eventually the campaign was dropped. Critics decried the fact that no dialogue ever took place to consider ways of reducing the tower's impact on the landscape.

The Seville Tower today is just one element in a rapidly developing area. Immediately to the north, for example, it has been joined by two boomerang-shaped, four-storey structures on stilts. Also designed by César Pelli, they contain a shopping plaza with eighty stores. Both structures have sloping roof gardens accessed by means of zig-zag paths. At the north end of the plaza is the CaixaForum Sevilla, a cultural and arts centre opened in 2017. Designed by architect Guillermo Vázquez Consuegra (b. 1945), it features a bold aluminium canopy beneath which is a single ground storey and two sub-levels reached by escalators.

The riverside fronting all these buildings has also been redeveloped as the Ferdinand Magellan Park (Parque Fernando Magallanes). Also by Consuegra, this consists of several hundred trees and is designed to be environmentally sustainable in that rainwater finds its way into the

The Torre Sevilla was Seville's first skyscraper

subsoil rather than running off into drains. Towards the northern end of the park is the Pabellón de la Navegación, a child-friendly maritime museum formed out of an earlier attraction created for Expo '92 (see no. 44). There is also the sleek Pasarela de Cartuja Bridge, again built for Expo '92, which is currently in the Guinness Book of Records as being the world's slimmest bridge in terms of the ratio between its length (771 feet) and width (36 feet).

Other locations nearby: 42, 44

44 The Remains of Expo '92

Isla de la Cartuja, a round walk through the former site
of Expo '92 beginning on Avenida Expo '92

London's Great Exhibition of 1851 was the first World Exposition. Defined as a large, general scope exhibition of up to six months' duration, such expositions have been hosted by a different city every few years since. In 1992 it was the turn of Seville, which took as its theme 'The Age of Discovery'. It marked the quincentenary of Christopher Columbus (1451–1506) setting sail from Spain to explore the New World.

Expo '92 was staged between April and October on the Isla de La Cartuja, part of a peninsula formed by two arms of the Guadalquivir River. It was the ideal spot in that it comprised not only 500 acres of empty land but also the former Carthusian monastery in which Columbus planned his journeys. When completed it consisted of 102 pavilions set in a vast man-made landscape of roads, gardens and water features. The homegrown pavilions were thematic – Navigation, Discovery, the 15th Century, Nature and the Environment – with separate pavilions celebrating Andalucia and Spain (the old monastery doubled as the Royal Pavilion). The other pavilions represented the various participating nations.

Expo '92 attracted almost 42 million visitors. When the event closed most pavilions were demolished, including the Japanese Pavilion, which at the time was the largest wooden structure in the world. Around thirty remained, however, which were subsequently reused or else abandoned. The following walk takes in a selection of them.

Starting on Avenida Expo '92, head northwards along Camino de los Descubrimientos (Way of Discoveries). Note as you go the river bridges built to provide access to the site, part of the citywide improvements that also gave Seville a new airport and railway station (see no. 27).

First on the right is the Navigation Pavilion (Pabellón de la Navegación), with its distinctive tower in the water. Today it contains a museum of maritime navigation. Next on the left is the former Carthusian Monastery, now a centre for Andalucian art (see no. 42). On the riverbank here is the jungle-like Jardin Americano planted with species introduced from the Americas.

At end of the gardens is a river inlet that fed a now reed-filled canal. This once conveyed visitors past the currently abandoned Auditorio de la Cartuja, the exquisite Moroccan Pavilion (Pabellón de Marruecos) (now a Mediterranean cultural foundation), and the fenced-off Future Pavilion (Pabellón del Futuro), with its unmissable *Ariane 4* rocket parked in front. At the end is the Modernist Spanish Pavilion (Pabellón de España), which backs onto a modern theme park, the Isla Mágica (Magic Island) (see no. 49).

Now turn left along Calle Isaac Newton to see the dozen white towers of the European Union Pavilion (Pabellón de la Unión Europea) (see front cover). Each represents a member nation at the time, with a multi-coloured central tower bearing their flags. Carry on to Calle de Leonardo da Vinci and turn left again to return to your starting point. En route you will pass the seven-spired Hungarian Pavilion (Pabellón de Hungria), the Bioclimatic Sphere, and the zinc-clad Canadian Pavilion (Pabellón de Canadá),

The European Union Pavilion (Pabellón de la Unión Europea) at the Expo '92 site

all Expo remnants, as well as the buildings of Cartuja 93, a new science and technology park constructed over the western reaches of the site.

For an unusual overview of the former Expo site visit the 150-foot-high Torre de Perdigones (Shot Tower) on Calle Resolana (La Macarena) (see page 118). Erected in 1885, it was originally used to manufacture gun shot by dripping molten lead from the top of the tower down through perforated screens. Today a camera obscura enables visitors to see live images of the surrounding areas.

Other locations nearby: 42, 43

45 Ghosts of the Inquisition

Triana, the Museum of the Castle of San Jorge (Museo Del Castillo De San Jorge) on Plaza del Altozano (note: the museum is currently closed for renovation)

Walking through the gardens of the Prado de San Sebastián is a pleasurable experience, with its avenues of trees and water features. Five hundred years ago, however, the scene would have been very different. Back then it was the setting for the *Quemadero*, a platform on which victims of the Inquisition were burned alive. The Inquisition was headquartered in the Castle of San Jorge (Castillo de San Jorge) across the river in Triana. It, too, is today a changed location, its fragmentary remains now concealed beneath a modern market.

Triana, a working-class district *(barrio obrero)* once home to potters, sailors, bullfighters and *flamenco* dancers, is reached by means of a fine 19th-century iron bridge, the Puente Isabelle II (see nos. 12, 41, 42). According to legend, Triana is named after the Roman Emperor Trajan (53–117 AD), who was born in the nearby Roman city of Itálica, although it may alternatively be derived from the Latin *Trans amnem* meaning 'those beyond the river'.

Where the bridge makes landfall in the Plaza del Altozano is Triana's market (Mercado de Triana). Open since 1822, its present incarnation has been in operation since 2001. It was during maintenance work in 1983 on an earlier iteration of the market that the remains of the infamous Castle of San Jorge were revealed, as well as those of the Almohad-era fortress and necropolis that preceded it.

With the old market in need of considerable additional work, the decision was taken in 1990 to demolish it completely. Before the present structure was built, however, archaeologists were given the chance to reveal as much of the castle as possible. Since 2009, with the ruins safely consolidated, the site has been open as the Museum of the Castle of San Jorge (Museo Del Castillo De San Jorge).

The museum documents the Inquisition's merciless 300-year purge of heretics and apostates from its arrival at the castle in 1481 until the execution of its last victim in 1781. As a state-sponsored religious tribunal, the Inquisition's main task was to ensure that converts to Catholicism were keeping the faith. Seville was its testing ground, where repression and fearmongering were commonplace, and interrogation methods including torture and brutality were perfected. Unique among them was the *auto-da-fé* (act of faith), a humiliating ritual of

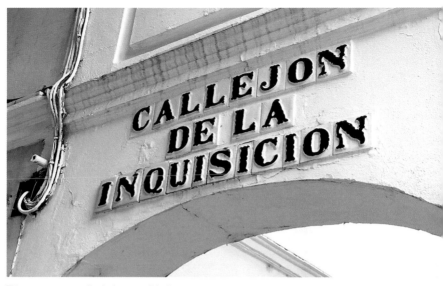

This street name recalls the horrors of the Inquisition

public penance after which the condemned was handed over to the civil authorities for punishment, the most severe of which was the *Quemadero*.

Of all those imprisoned and tortured in the castle, Seville's Jews probably suffered the most. Despite having been forcibly converted to Catholicism many were still outed as being *marranos*, that is converts *(conversos)* who continued to practise Judaism in secret (see no. 10). As visitors to the museum walk through the remains of jail cells, stables, domestic quarters and the home of the Grand Inquisitor, they will learn of what happened here three centuries ago and no doubt leave with some unsettling emotions. It is the pathetic state of the ruins today in their banal setting compared with the magnitude of the crime they witnessed that makes the place so very affecting (should the museum be closed, an unassuming stretch of castle wall can be seen from inside the present market building).

After leaving the museum and returning to pavement level take a look around the back of the market building. A narrow brick-vaulted alleyway between Calle Callao and Calle Castilla is called Callejon de la Inquisition. Prisoners were once led this way and today it is the only evidence above ground that the Inquisition was ever here.

Other locations nearby: 46, 47

46 The Andalucian Kitchen

Triana, a selection of traditional restaurants including Casa Cuesta at Calle Castilla 1 (note: Casa Cuesta is open all day although many restaurants close after lunch and don't re-open until 8pm)

With roots stretching back to Moorish times, the Andalucian kitchen is as varied as the region's terrain: fish caught in the Mediterannean and Atlantic, fruit and vegetables sun-ripened on the plains, meat and game from the wooded hills. With such an abundance of locally-sourced ingredients, it is little wonder that Andalucia's traditional recipes remain popular with locals and visitors alike.

When enjoying Andalucian food it is useful to understand Spanish eating habits. On weekdays Spaniards tend to make lunch (almuerzo) their main meal. Enjoyed around 2pm, when offices close for *siesta*, it is often eaten out on weekdays. Dinner (La Cena) in a restaurant is usually reserved for the weekends and starts famously late around 8.30pm. The atmosphere is always convivial with friends and family in tow.

Lunch and dinner (as opposed to *tapas*) often starts with soups *(sopas)*, salads *(ensaladas)*, eggs and omelettes *(huevos y tortillas)*, and vegetable dishes *(verduras y legumbres)*. A signature starter is *gazpacho*, a cold soup made from fresh tomatoes, cucumbers and peppers. Main courses fall into two categories: fish and seafood *(pescados y mariscos)* or meat and game *(carnes y aves)*. Despite Seville being inland, it is connected to the sea by the Guadalquivir River, so there is always something on the menu for pescatarians, including the Spanish favourite, *paella* (the Moors introduced this dish's all-important rice and bay leaves). Meat, however, is more prevalent, with beef *(ternera)* and lamb *(cordero)* popular. Pork *(cerdo)* is the real king though and it comes in all forms from the famous cured Iberian hams *(Jamón Ibérico)* and sausages *(salchichas)* to braised pork cheeks *(carilladas)* and tenderloin *(solomillo)* served in various sauces. Desserts *(postres)* are available but fresh fruit *(fruta)* is preferred due to its abundance and Seville's summer heat.

An atmospheric place in which to sample traditional Andalucian cuisine is Casa Cuesta at Calle Castilla 1 (Triana). Established in 1880, this combined restaurant, bar and café is the last of eleven taverns that once lined the street between here and the Triana Bridge. Today it features a sturdy marble-topped bar, wooden wine shelves, polychrome wall tiles and vintage bullfighting posters. The ceramic wall advertisement for *Caballero* brandy adds to the scene.

The chefs at Casa Cuesta pride themselves on following and updating handwritten recipes used in the kitchen in the 1920s. Order a *fino* sherry or a *tinto de verano* (red wine mixed with lemonade) and let them prepare a feast for you: fried eggplant fingers drizzled with honey *(Berenjenas con miel)* for starters perhaps, followed by pork cheek stew marinaded in Andalucian Pedro Ximénez sherry, or for vegetarians, the Arab-influenced spinach and chickpea stew. Ingredients are sourced locally, including the best Andalucian olive oil.

Traditional food and drink at Casa Cuesta in Triana

Seville has many traditional restaurants. In Santa Cruz these include El Modesto at Calle Cano y Cueto 5, where good paella is served overlooking the Jardines de Murillo, and Méson Don Raimundo at Calle Argote de Molino 26, which specialises in poultry and game. Over in La Macarena is La Quinta Braseria at Plaza Padre Jerónimo de Córdoba 11 serving excellent chicken croquettes (croquetas de pollo) in an old townhouse. And nearer the river, in El Arenal, is El Burladero at Calle Canalejas 1, which specialises in oxtail *(cola de toro)* dishes served against a backdrop of bullfighting memorabilia. Also here is the elegant Taberna del Alabardero at Calle Zaragoza 20, which should be good as it is the home of Seville's Hospitality High School (Escuela Superior de Hostelería).

Other locations nearby: 45, 47

47   A Centre for Ceramics

Triana, the Centro Cerámica Triana at Calle Callao 16

The district of Triana on the west bank of the Guadalquivir River was once described as a neighbourhood of bullfighters, sailors and *flamenco* dancers. Today these historic communities have disappeared and even Triana's famous potters have gone elsewhere. They have, however, left a glorious visual legacy in the form of decorative tilework on many of the districts's buildings. Moreover their work is now celebrated in a fine museum, the Centro Cerámica Triana.

There is good reason why a ceramics' industry grew up in Triana. The necessary raw materials – water and clay – are provided abundantly by the Guadalquivir. The clay particularly, known as *barro* ('mud'), has a texture ideal for moulding. The Romans and the Moors were the first to appreciate this and by the 12th-century kilns were operating here in the shadow of an Almohad-era fortress (see no. 45).

Moorish artisans deployed techniques imported from Morocco, including decoarative brickwork and geometrically-arranged glazed tiles. The tiles, known as *azulejos* (from the Arabic *az-zulayj* meaning 'little stone'), were not only durable and colourful but also kept rooms cool in the summer. Their use persisted long after the Reconquest as part of the Mudéjar (Christian Moorish) tradition (see no. 1).

The art of *azulejos* continued to evolve in Triana. By the 15th and 16th centuries, new decorative techniques were being employed. These included an Italian process whereby pictures were painted across multiple varnished tiles, and another in which images were stamped onto individual tiles while the clay was still damp. Industrialisation brought further changes, with *azulejos* mass-produced in factories.

All this and more is illustrated in the Centro Cerámica Triana, a museum housed suitably in the former Cerámica Santa Ana factory at Calle Callao 16. Using historical artefacts and multimedia techniques, the four key ingredients in the ceramic process are illustrated: mud from the riverbank; water to knead it into clay; fire to heat the kilns; and air for drying the finished products. Some of the factory's round kilns dating back to the 16th century still survive, alongside more recent ones named after famous Triana bullfighters. They are accompanied by other important pieces of equipment, including basins in which the pigments used to colour the tiles were ground and mixed. Videos of a boy kneading clay with his feet, and artisans hand-painting tiles, are reminders of how labour intensive the original process was.

The Centro Cerámica celebrates Triana's pottery heritage

Up on the first floor there is a marvellous gallery of ceramics created in the potteries of Triana (see inside back cover). They range from Moorish terracottas and Renaissance painted figurative scenes to Mudéjar geometric azulejos and 20th century trade advertisements. Also displayed are products from the renowned Pickman factory at the nearby La Cartuja monastery (see no. 42).

Wonderful ceramics can be found in the streets surrounding the museum. They include the belfry of the Iglesia de Nuestra Señora de la O at Calle Castilla 30, street altars outside the Iglesia de San Jacinto at Calle Pagés del Corro 88, and the pretty Capilla del Carmen on the Triana Bridge. Secular examples include road and shop signs, entrance halls in taverns and private homes, and trade signs. And don't miss the former Montalván ceramics' factory at Calle Alfareria 21, which now functions as a hotel. Like the Santa Ana factory, its tiled façade once acted as a huge visual catalogue of the company's products.

Other locations nearby: 45, 46

48 A Most Famous Fair

Los Remedios, the Seville Fair (Feria de Sevilla) at the Real de la Feria between Los Remedios and Tablada (note: the fair takes place annually two weeks after Easter)

Visit a traditional Sevillian *tapas* bar and the chances are it will be decorated with vintage posters. These will often depict women in frilled *flamenco* dresses and men on horseback accompanied by the words *Feria de Sevilla* (Seville Fair) The fair is one of the city's great annual events, when Sevillians indulge in the customs for which they are famous.

During the Middle Ages, Seville held two annual fairs for farmers and artisans. By the 19th century, however, both were discontinued. So it was that in 1847 two enterprising men from northern Spain gained approval from the 15-year-old Queen Isabella II (1830–1904) to stage a new fair. Initially a horse fair, it was held at the Prado de San Sebastián. By the following year it had taken on a festive atmosphere thanks to the temporary erection of three large decorated tents *(casetas)* belonging to the Duke and Duchess of Montpensier, the Town Hall, and the Casino of Seville. With admission by invitation *(enchufe)* only, it was in these *casetas* that the fun of the fair continued after hours.

By the 1920s, prominent families, trade associations, clubs and political parties were all hosting their own *casetas* transforming the fair into the colourful social spectacle it is today. Since 1973, the seven-day fair has been held at the Real de la Feria, a bespoke site located between the neighbourhoods of Los Remedios and Tablada. Covering twenty four blocks and criss-crossed by streets named for famous bullfighters, the vast space now hosts over a thousand *casetas*.

The fair takes place two weeks after Easter Holy Week (Semana Santa) hence its formal name, the Seville April Fair (Feria de abril de Sevilla) (see no. 38). Celebrations officially start at midnight on Saturday with the *alumbrao*. This is when people gather in front of the decorative main gate *(portada)* built especially for that year's fair and watch its myriad coloured lights switched on. They then enter the fair grounds to dine at one of the *casetas* either by invitation or else in one of the designated public tents. Fish is the traditional dish so the evening is also referred to as *Noche del Pescaíto* (Night of the Fish).

Thereafter, each day of the fair begins at midday with a parade of horsedrawn carriages, a reflection of Seville's long equestrian tradition, with riders in ornate tailored outfits. The carriages first make

A poster from the 1930s advertising the famous Seville Fair

their way to the Plaza de Toros de la Maestranza bullring (El Arenal), where they are judged for their beauty and condition. Bullfighting is also an integral part of the fair and the bullfighting season kicks off at the same time (see no. 26).

Later the carriages make their way to the fairground, where from around 9pm until early the next morning, Sevillians sip sherry, eat *tapas* and dance the *Sevillanas*, a popular dance with a *flamenco* accent. The women are especially resplendent in their showy dresses accessorised with shawls, veils and hair combs. Younger participants inevitably gravitate towards the noisy amusement park – the aptly-named Calle del Infierno (Hell Road) – erected temporarily nearby, as well as the circus in the adjacent Parque de los Príncipes.

To purchase vintage *feria* posters, visit FÉLIX at Plaza de Cabildo 7 (El Arenal). For a range of *feria* dress accessories try Juan Foronda at Calle Sierpes 33 (Santa Cruz) and Juan Osete at Calle de Castilla 10 (Triana).

49 In the Wake of Magellan

Parque de María Luisa, the Seville Aquarium (Acuario de Sevilla) on Muelle de las Delicias

In 2019, Seville celebrated the 500th anniversary of the first circumnavigation of the earth. The Portuguese explorer Ferdinand Magellan (1480–1521) set sail from the city in 1519 with a fleet of five ships. Three years later the carrack *Victoria* captained by Juan Sebastián Elcano (1476–1526) returned safely to Spain, Magellan having perished en route. A monument to the men's achievements in the form of a large armillary sphere was erected in the Plaza de Cuba (Los Remedios), formerly the site of the Las Mulas pier from where the expedition departed.

Elsewhere in Seville, Magellan and Elcano's achievement is recalled in a different way. The superb Seville Aquarium (Acuario de Sevilla), which opened in 2014 on Muelle de las Delicias (Parque de María Luisa), is uniquely organised into five zones representing the five aquatic ecosystems through which the expedition passed.

The first zone covers the Guadalquivir, Andalucia's longest river, which connects Seville to the Atlantic. Having departed Seville on August 10th 1519, Magellan's fleet descended it to reach Sanlúcar de Barrameda from where on September 20th it sailed south-west to Tenerife. The creatures inhabiting the river, both native and invasive, are represented, with special attention given to the denizens of the marshy Doñana National Park.

The second zone covers the Atlantic, which Magellan traversed via the Canary Islands to reach the east coast of South America. Covering twenty percent of the planet's surface, the Atlantic contains many habitats – from sandy shallows to deep water trenches – all of which are represented here. It took Magellan almost four months to reach South America, the focus of the third zone, which includes the Amazon and its remarkably diverse tropical rainforests. Whilst cruising along the coastline, he coined the place name Patagonia on account of its tall inhabitants, Patagón being an oversized character in Spanish literature.

Next Magellan reached the Pacific, where he discovered new lands, including the Philippines. It was there that he was killed during a skirmish with local tribesmen. This vast body of water, which contains some of the ocean's largest creatures, is covered by the aquarium's fourth zone. Here visitors can watch huge sea turtles and sharks swimming freely in a 30-foot-deep tank.

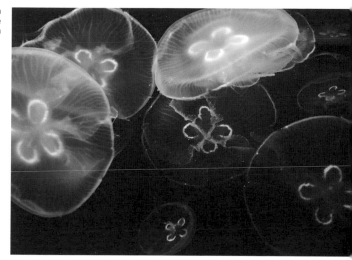

Mesmerising jellyfish at the Seville Aquarium

The fifth and final zone represents the Indo-Pacific, where the Indian and Pacific oceans meet. Now under the command of Elcano, whose monument stands not far from the aquarium on the Glorieta de los Marineros roundabout, the expedition toured various tropical islands, including the Moluccas. There they loaded up with spices such as nutmeg and cloves before returning home. The creatures on display occupy coral reefs and mangrove swamps, with a special room devoted entirely to jellyfish. Accompanied by piped music and minimal lighting, the experience is hypnotic. There is also a window looking directly into the aquarium's jellyfish reproduction facility.

History aside, the Seville Aquarium conducts important on- and off-site conservation and research programmes. It also has an active outreach programme hosting exciting school activities, courses for students and teachers' days. Adults can even sign up for romantic dinners served up alongside the illuminated fishtanks!

Children who enjoy the aquarium will also enjoy the Isla Mágica, a theme park on Seville's former Expo '92 site recreating the exploits of Seville's 16th century maritime explorers (see no. 44). More serious is the Museo Casa de la Ciencia on Avenida de María Luisa (Parque de María Luisa), a science and education centre occupying the former Peru Pavilion (Pabellón de Perú) of the Ibero-American Exposition of 1929 (Exposición iberoamericana de 1929).

Other locations nearby: 50, 51, 52, 53

50 The Treasure of El Carambolo

Parque de María Luisa, the Archaeological Museum
(Museo Arqueológico) in the Fine Arts Pavilion (Pabellón
de Bellas Artes) at Plaza América 51 (note: the museum
is currently closed for renovation)

Andalucia is a region rich in archaeology, with distinct Iberian cultures identified from the Neolithic period onwards. The Phoenicians, Greeks, Romans and Visigoths followed before the arrival of the Moors, and each have left their mark. In Seville the place to find out about them is the Archaeological Museum (Museo Arqueológico) at Plaza América 51 (Parque de María Luisa).

The museum is housed in one of several pavilions designed for the Ibero-American Exposition of 1929 (Exposición iberoamericana de 1929) (see nos. 20, 51). Originally called the Fine Arts Pavilion (Pabellón de Bellas Artes), its neo-Renaissance style reflected the penchant of local architect Aníbal González (1876–1929) for Revivalist styles. Since 1942, the building has served as the headquarters of the Archaeological Museum of Seville.

The museum's holdings are extensive ranging from the Palaeolithic up to and including the Middle Ages. It seems fitting that the oldest artefacts are to be found in the basement. Here the pre-Roman era is generously represented with Stone Age hand tools, Neolithic pottery and Phoenician clay goddesses. The real highlight though is the so-called Treasure of El Carambolo (Tesoro del Carambolo). This hoard of goldwork is thought to be representative of the indigenous but little-understood Tartessos Culture, which appears in the archaeological record between the 9th and 6th centuries BC.

The treasure was unearthed by construction workers in 1958 on El Carambolo, a hill in the Camas municipality west of Seville. It comprises twenty one pieces of finely-crafted, locally-sourced gold: a necklace with pendants, two bracelets, two ox-hide-shaped pectorals, and sixteen plaques that most likely formed a necklace or diadem. Thought to have been deliberately buried in the 6th century (but manufactured as early as the 8th), it is unclear whether the objects formed a hoard or else were perhaps attached to textiles adorning animals in some cultic sacrifice.

Two distinct sites have been identified at El Carambolo: an earlier one reflecting a purely indigenous (presumably Tartessian) culture; and a later one dating from the mid-8th century and the beginning of trade with the Phoenicians. The treasure, which shows clear Phoeni-

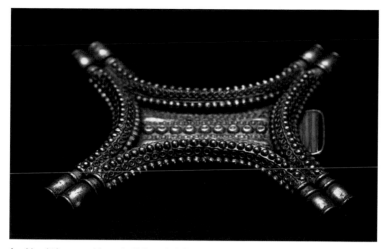

A gold ox-hide pectoral from the El Carambolo Treasure

cian influences, is associated with the later site and may have been buried when the site was destroyed in the 6th century. However, it remains a moot point among archaeologists as to whether the treasure and indeed the site was ever more Tartessian than Phoenician.

The discussion has not been helped by the fact that Tartessos itself has yet to be found. One possible candidate is Huelva some sixty miles west of Seville on the Gulf of Cádiz. Called Onuba by the Phoenicians, it would certainly fit the description by Herodotus that Tartessos lay beyond the Pillars of Hercules (as the Straits of Gibraltar were known). Other commentators use the fact that the name 'Tartessos' dies out during the Greek period as proof that the settlement, wherever it may have been, was lost to coastal flooding.

Upstairs in the museum the main galleries cover the Roman era, with architectural fragments, glass and ceramics from Hispalis (Roman Seville), Itálica and other Roman settlements (see no. 30). Highlights include a marble colossus of Trajan, who together with Hadrian was born in Itálica. Unmissable is the magnificent 3rd century BC mosaic from Écija called the *Triumph of Bacchus* in which the God of Wine is shown returning from India in a chariot. The museum's other galleries cover early Christian sarcophagi, Visigothic relics and finds from Moorish Spain, including artefacts from the 10th century palace of Medina Azahara.

Other locations nearby: 49, 51, 52, 53

51 Barrels, Lace and Castanets

Parque de María Luisa, the Museum of Popular Arts and Customs (Museo de Artes y Costumbres Populares) in the Mudéjar Pavilion (Pabellón Mudéjar) at Plaza de América 3

Anyone interested in the traditions of old Andalucia should visit the Museum of Popular Arts and Customs (Museo de Artes y Costumbres Populares). Housed in one of the pavilions built for the Ibero-American Exposition of 1929 (Exposición iberoamericana de 1929), this diverse collection covers everything from the intricacies of lace manufacture to the tools required to make castanets *(castañuelas)*.

Completed in 1914 on the Plaza América (Parque de María Luisa), the pavilion was one of several in the park designed by local architect Aníbal González (1876–1929). His penchant for Revivalist styles is apparent in the name of the building: the Mudéjar Pavilion (Pabellón Mudéjar). Whereas elsewhere he opted for neo-Gothic or neo-Renaissance styles, here he deployed an idiom known as neo-*Mudéjar* in which 16th century Christian Moorish forms were reinvented for the 19th and 20th centuries (see no. 20). Thus, the building's exposed brick exterior is enlivened with Moroccan-style ceramic tiles *(azulejos)*, the doors have polylobed arches typical of Moorish Andalucia, and at the corners of the building are mock minarets (see back cover).

During the Exposition, the pavilion served as an art gallery known as the Pavilion of Ancient Art and Artistic Industries (Pabellón de Arte Antiguo e Industrias Artísticas). Since then, the inside of the building has been remodelled, with a new first floor inserted and a spiral staircase installed. The Museum of Popular Arts and Customs, which opened in 1973, occupies the ground floor, first floor and basement, with a library, restoration room and photographic studio at the top of the building.

The museum's diverse holdings ome from a variety of sources. The ground floor, for example, is largely taken up with one of Europe's finest collections of embroidery and lace. Numbering almost 6,000 pieces, it was donated by (and named for) the Díaz Velázquez family. Accompanying the collection is a recreation of the family's home. Other named collections include the Aguiar collection of *costumbrismo* paintings (pictorial depictions of everyday Hispanic life and customs) and the Loty collection of over 2,000 glass panels depicting Andalucian cities between 1900 and 1936.

Up on the first floor there are displays pertaining to religious art, musical instruments, and embroidery. Beautiful as they are, these exhibits lack their original context, as is so often the case in museums. This is remedied, however, in the museum's basement, where eight complete craft workshops have been saved and reconstructed in their entirety. They include those of Claudio Bernal, Seville's last maker of wooden barrels, guitarmaker Francisco Barber, goldsmith Fernando Marmolejo, whose family worked gold in Seville for over 400 years, master castanet maker Filigrana, and gilders José Jiménez and Manuel Calvo. The other workshops cover saddlemaking, pottery and china painting. Subsidiary displays cover furniture making, wickerwork, leatherworking, winemaking and gunsmithing. Of particular interest is the display relating to the history of Andalucian ceramics and glazed tiles *(azulejos)*. Seville has been a centre of this craft since Moorish times (see no. 47).

A castanet maker's workshop at the Museum of Popular Arts and Customs

One final exhibit with a uniquely Seville focus is the Mencos Collection. The world's most comprehensive assemblage of posters, lithographs and photographs relating to the annual Seville Fair (Feria de Sevilla) and Easter Holy Week (Semana Santa), it also embraces *flamenco* and bullfighting.

The Mudéjar Pavilion has appeared several times on the big screen. In *The Wind and the Lion* (1975) it doubles as the Pasha's palace in Tangier, when it is assaulted by American troops. In the French film *Harem* (1985) it stands in for the British Embassy, whilst in *Lawrence of Arabia* (1962) it is portrayed as being in Jerusalem.

Other locations nearby: 49, 50, 52, 53

52 The Queen's Sewing Box

Parque de María Luisa, the Queen's Sewing Box (Costurero de la Reina) at Paseo de las Delicias 9 (note: the building can only be seen from the outside)

One of Seville's quirkiest buildings goes by the name of Costurero de la Reina or Queen's Sewing Box. Built in the form of a miniature hexagonal castle, it stands in a corner of the Parque de María Luisa, where its name reflects an enduring legend.

Despite its vaguely Moorish appearance, the building only dates back to the late-19th century. At that time the area was part of the extensive gardens of the Palacio de San Telmo. This huge Baroque palace on Avenida de Roma was owned by Antoine d'Orléans, Duke of Montpensier (1824–1890), youngest son of the exiled French King Louis Philippe I (1773–1850) (see no. 36). The Duke's death in 1890 left the palace and gardens in the hands of his wife, the Infanta María Luisa Fernanda (1832–1897), and it was she who in 1893 oversaw construction of the Costurero de la Reina.

The building is certainly striking, with its triangular crenelations, corner towers, Moorish-style windows and horizontal-striped paintwork. But what makes it unique is that it was the first building in Seville to be rendered in the so-called neo-*Mudéjar* style in which Christian Moorish forms of the 16th century were revived for a modern audience. Although the architect most often associated with this style is Aníbal González (1876–1929), the Costurero de la Reina was designed by Juan Talavera y de la Vega (1832–1905), an architect long associated with the Duke of Montpensier and his wife. His only other neo-*Mudéjar* work of note is a private villa, the Casa Mensaque on Calle San Jacinto (Triana), which also features horizontal-striped paintwork.

More neo-*Mudéjar* buildings joined the Costurero de la Reina after the Infanta willed her gardens to the City of Seville, which were renamed in her honour. Mostly designed by Aníbal González, they acted as pavilions for the Ibero-American Exposition of 1929 (Exposición iberoamericana de 1929) (see no. 20).

Considering the fact that the Costurero de la Reina was built as a garden house it's worth explaining how it became erroneously associated with a queen and her sewing. In 1872 the Duke of Montpensier's daughter, Maria de las Mercedes d'Orléans (1860–1878), met her first cousin, King Alfonso XII (1857–1885). The two were married in 1878 although the happy union ended after only six months when Maria

The quirky Queen's Sewing Box in the Parque de María Luisa

succumbed to typhoid. According to popular tradition Maria spent the years prior to her marriage sewing in the garden house at the Palacio de San Telmo giving rise to its popular name name of Costurero de la Reina or Queen's Sewing Box. The scene is intensified by tales of Alfonso arriving on horseback from the Alcázar of Seville to woo her. This, however, is clearly impossible as we know Maria died a full fifteen years before the building was constructed! It nevertheless makes for a charming tale.

A little further north from the Queen's Sewing Box is the Seville Public Library inaugurated in 1999 by the Infanta Elena, Duchess of Lugo (b. 1963). The sleek two-story building conceals an interior courtyard, quite invisible from the outside, which provides a source of natural light for the reading rooms. The courtyard itself doubles as an *al fresco* reading area. In 2001 the building was nominated for the Mies van der Rohe Award for European Architecture. Further north still, on the river bank, is a large but little-known outdoor mosaic depicting the course of the Guadalquivir from source to sea.

Other locations nearby: 49, 50, 51, 53, 54, 55

53 The Plaza de España

Parque de María Luisa, the Plaza de España

If one had to cite a modern counterpart to Seville Cathedral it would surely be the Plaza de España. Every bit as splendid but built for secular reasons, it formed the centrepiece of the city's Ibero-American Exposition of 1929 (Exposición iberoamericana de 1929). Today it is marvelled at by visitors for its fantasy architecture, eye-popping ceramics and historical symbolism.

The idea for an Ibero-American Exposition celebrating Spain and its former colonies was proposed as early as 1909. As plans came together, the organising committee proposed creating a large public arena in which to host ceremonies and events. Its monumental design would be emblematic of the exposition as a whole, whilst also acting as the headquarters of the host country.

Dubbed the Plaza de España, the structure was located at the northern end of the Parque de María Luisa. It was designed by Aníbal González (1876–1929), a Seville-born architect who had given up Modernism in favour of Historicism. This revivalist style celebrated architectural styles that had triumphed in bygone Andalucia, namely Gothic, *Mudéjar* (Christian Moorish), Renaissance and Baroque. By deploying them in the present, onlookers would be reminded of Spain's historical glories. The style also celebrated contemporary local craft techniques in the form of painted glazed ceramics *(azulejos)*, exposed brickwork and wrought iron, hence it also being termed Sevillian Regionalism or *Andalucismo*.

González designed many of the pavilions that made up the Exposition but the Plaza de España was his masterpiece (see no. 20). It comprises a spacious semi-circular plaza some 660 feet in diameter, surrounded by a canal running for a third of a mile and crossed by four tiled footbridges, with cast iron lamp standards at each end. The plaza's backdrop is provided by an imposing crescent of buildings in a mish-mash of Gothic, *Mudéjar* and Renaissance styles, terminated at each end by neo-Baroque towers. Each with a height of 240 feet, these are inspired by the towers of Santiago de Compostella.

That construction lasted from 1914 until 1928 is indicative not only of the work involved but also of the high cost, both of which caused delays. Fortunately, González was assisted in his herculean task by fellow architect Aurelio Gómez Millán (1898–1991), engineer José Luis de Casso Romero and over a thousand labourers.

The Plaza de España was imbued with much symbolism. The semi-circular design, for example, represented Spain embracing its former colonies, and the orientation towards the Guadalquivir, referenced the river that carried mariners and merchants to the Americas. The four bridges crossing the canal represented the four ancient kingdoms of Spain – Asturias, Castile, Galicia and León. Additionally, the crescent had at its foot a series of alcoves representing the forty eight Spanish provinces, each covered in *azulejos* depicting key events in their history. The curious shelved 'lanterns' either side of each alcove originally contained promotional literature extolling the virtues of each province.

The Plaza de España built for the Ibero-American Exposition of 1929

The crescent today is home to a variety of official organisations, as well as a small but informative Military History Museum beneath the northern tower. Its holdings range from models of the defences of various Andalucian towns to full-size artillery pieces.

Science fiction fans probably know that the Plaza de España appears in the *Star Wars* film *Attack of the Clones* (2002), in which it doubles as the city of Theed on the planet Naboo. In *Lawrence of Arabia* (1962) it stands in for British Army headquarters in Cairo.

Other locations nearby: 49, 50, 51, 52, 54, 55

54 Where Carmen Rolled Cigars

Parque de María Luisa, the former Royal Tobacco Factory (Real Fábrica de Tabacos) on Calle San Fernando

Seville is surely the only city with a university housed in a former tobacco factory and it's no ordinary factory. Not only is the building on Calle San Fernando (Parque de María Luisa) a masterpiece of Sevillian Baroque architecture but it also provided the backdrop for one of the world's best-known operas.

The Royal Tobacco Factory (Real Fábrica de Tabacos) was built during the reign of King Charles III (1716–1788), a Bourbon monarch of the Enlightenment. Completed in 1771 to a design by Brussels-born architect Sebastián Van der Borcht (b. 1725), the vast building is formed around a dozen internal courtyards. Measuring 600 feet square, it is Spain's second largest building after the El Escorial in Madrid. Despite its practical function, however, it was a refined structure, with Baroque detailing on all four sides, ornate entrance portals and inside elegant arcades, a chapel and a fountain. The factory was also something of a fortress designed to protect the king's highly lucrative monopoly on tobacco. This explains the moat on three sides crossed by drawbridges, the watchtowers at each corner and even a secret canal to convey tobacco by barge from galleons moored on the nearby river. It also accounts for the prison in which anyone caught smuggling tobacco out of the building was incarcerated.

At its height the factory employed over 3000 female cigar makers *(cigarreras)*, the world's largest ever female urban proletariat. They had a reputation for being both headstrong and sensual, with "carnations in their hair and daggers in their garters". During the 19th century three quarters of the cigars smoked in Europe were rolled on these admirable women's laps.

During the 19th century the factory became an unlikely visitor attraction for travellers in search of Romantic Spain. Intrigued by the mix of hard graft and passion, their quest was fuelled by French author Prosper Mérimée (1803–1870) in his novella *Carmen* (1845). It concerns the gypsy *cigarerra* Carmen, who turns her sensual gaze from a smitten soldier, José, to a daring bullfighter, Lucas, only to be murdered by her spurned former lover. Mérimée's book became hugely successful in 1875, when it formed the basis of an opera of the same name by Georges Bizet (1838–1875). The popular *habanera* aria is set outside the factory. Later, in 1915, the Spanish *costumbrista* painter

Las Cigarerras (1915) by Gonzalo Bilbao Martínez

Gonzalo Bilbao Martínez (1860–1938) depicted women like Carmen at work in the factory in his atmospheric painting *Las Cigarreras* (The Cigar Makers). It hangs today in Seville's Museum of Fine Arts (Museo de Bellas Artes).

Only in the 1950s was tobacco production relocated across the river to the Altadis Tobacco Factory on Calle de Sebastiàn Elcano. The old factory then became part of Seville University (Universidad de Sevilla), whilst the new factory (now also closed) is being reworked as an arts' centre.

The old factory today can be entered from the main portal on Calle San Fernando, which is decorated with boats and busts of Columbus and Cortès, references to the 16th century discovery of tobacco in South America. It is, however, difficult to imagine today's minimalist interior bustling with the *cigarreras* of old as they brought bundles of sun-dried tobacco leaves down from the roof for shredding and rolling into cigars.

A less well-known historic factory in Seville is the Royal Artillery Factory on Avenida de Eduardo Dato (San Bernardino). Built in 1565 and rebuilt in 1720, it was Spain's main armaments factory for several centuries and remained in use until 1991. The huge vaulted structure is currently being refurbished as a cultural and innovation centre.

Other locations nearby: 24, 52, 53, 55

55 Hotels with History

Parque de María Luisa, a selection of historic hotels including the Hotel Alfonso XIII at Calle San Fernando 2

Some of Seville's most enchanting cultural attractions are its historic palaces. Many visitors are captivated by their arcaded, flower-filled *patios*, echoing to the sound of tinkling fountains. Some no doubt dream how it would be to live in such lovely places. For them Seville offers numerous historic hotels where for a few precious days they can do just that.

The finest of them is undoubtedly the Hotel Alfonso XIII at Calle San Fernando 2 (Parque de María Luisa). Occupying its own landscaped garden, it was built to accommodate visitors to the Ibero–American Exposition of 1929 (Exposición iberoamericana de 1929) and named for the monarch of the day. With its decorative wrought iron and brickwork, it is a good example of the-then fashionable style known as Sevillian Regionalist or *Andalucismo* (see no. 20). Centre stage is the hotel's magnificent neo-*Mudéjar* (Christian Moorish Revival) *patio* surrounded by tiled arcades, which non-residents are welcome to explore before enjoying a drink at the elegant bar.

Seville has several other grand hotels designed to make guests feel like royalty. One of them is the Hotel Palacio Villapanés at Calle Santiago 31 (Santa Cruz). This converted 18th century Baroque palace also has a traditional arcaded *patio*, which lies beyond the ornate wrought iron gates. Additionally the hotel offers two smaller *patios*: the Patio de las Conchas, with its shell-encrusted fountain, and the Patio de los Naranjos, filled with fragrant potted orange trees.

Another 18th century property is the Hotel Simón at Calle García de Vinuesa 19 (El Arenal). Converted in 1870, its rooms and patios have played host to famous musicians, writers and athletes. Most famous of them all was the superstar matador Manolete (1917–1947), who died young after being fatally gored in the bullring at Linares (see no. 26).

For something more intimate but still with a touch of glamour try the Legado Alcázar at Calle Mariana de Pineda 18 (Santa Cruz). This stylish boutique hotel is built up against the walls of the Real Alcázar so that several of its rooms overlook the lush palace gardens. Inside several historic features are preserved, including a Moorish well, 17th century pottery jars and antique ceramic tiling, which provide satisfying counterpoints to the smart contemporary décor.

Luxury awaits the fortunate few at the Hotel Alfonso XIII

Another noteable boutique hotel is La Casa del Maestro at Calle Niño Ricardo 5 (Santa Cruz). The hotel and street name are both tributes to the great flamenco guitarist and composer Niño Ricardo (1904–1972), who once lived here. After his death his family converted the house into a hotel, with eleven rooms decorated with a musical theme.

Yet another boutique hotel with history is the Hotel Sacristía de Santa Ana (La Macarena). It occupies a converted 18th century mansion and features an arcaded patio with a Moorish-style fountain. It is decorated with replica Roman amphorae and even real Roman columns unearthed in the cellar. In keeping with the archaeological theme, the bedrooms are each named after a mythological figure.

This hotel selection finishes with the Hotel Inglaterra at Plaza Nueva 7 (El Arenal). Despite its modern appearance today, it is actually one of Seville's oldest hotels having opened in 1857 as the Fonda Inglaterra on the site of a demolished convent. Considered the city's finest place to stay before the construction of the Hotel Alfonso XIII, it has numbered author Hans Christian Anderson (1805–1875), composer Giuseppe Verdi (1813–1901) and England's Prince of Wales (1865–1936) among its guests.

Other locations nearby: 24, 52, 53, 54

Opening Times

Correct at time of going to press but should be checked before setting out.

Andalusian Centre of Contemporary Art (Centro Andaluz e Arte Contemporáneo), Monastery of La Cartuja (Monasterio de Santa Mariá de las Cuevas) (Isla de la Cartuja), Calle Américo Vespucio 2, Tue–Sat 11am–9pm, Sun 10am–3.30pm

Archaeological Museum (Museo Arqueológico) (Parque de María Luisa), Fine Arts Pavilion (Pabellón de Bellas Artes), Plaza América 51, currently closed for renovation

Bar El Comercio (Santa Cruz), Calle Lineros 9, Mon–Fri 7.30am–9pm, Sat 8am–9pm

Basílica de la Macarena (La Macarena), Plaza de la Esperanza Macarena, Mon–Sat 9am–2pm, 5–9pm, Sun 9.30am–2pm, 5–9pm

Casa Cuesta (Triana), Calle Castilla 1, Mon–Fri 8am–12.30am, Sat 8.30am–12.30am, Sun 9am–12.30am

Casa de Pilatos (Santa Cruz), Plaza de Pilatos 1, daily 9am–6pm

Casa Moreno (El Arenal), Calle Gamazo 7, Mon & Tue 9am–4pm, Wed–Fri 9am–4pm, 8–11pm, Sat 12.30pm–4pm, 8–11pm

Centro Cerámica Triana (Triana), Calle Callao 16, daily 10am–6pm

Cervecería Giralda (Santa Cruz), Calle Mateos Gago 1, 12pm–12am

City Hall (Ayuntamiento) (Santa Cruz), Plaza Nueva 1, guided tours only Mon & Wed–Thu 9am–2pm & 4–6pm, Fri 9am–2pm

Convento de Santa Paula (La Macarena), Calle Santa Paula 11, daily 9.30am–1pm, 5–6.45pm (ring doorbell for admission)

Corralón de Pelicano (La Macarena), Plaza Pelícano 4, individual opening times vary

El Rinconcillo (La Macarena), Calle Gerona 40, Wed–Sun 1–5.30pm, 8pm–12.30am

Flamenco Museum (Museo del Baile Flamenco) (Santa Cruz), Calle Manuel Rojas Marcos 3, daily 11am–6pm (first Sun of the month 4–6pm)

General Archive of the Indies (Archivo General de Indias) (Santa Cruz), Avenida de la Constitución, Tue–Sat 9.30am–4.30pm, Sun 10.30am–1.30pm

Hospital de los Venerables Sacerdotes (Santa Cruz), 8 Plaza Venerables, Tue–Sat 10am–7pm, Sun 10am–3pm

Iglesia de San Luis de los Franceses (Santa Cruz), Calle San Luis 37, Tue–Sun 10am–2pm, 4–8pm

Iglesia de Santa María la Blanca (Santa Cruz), Calle Santa María la Blanca 5, Mon–Sat 10am–1pm, 6–10.30pm (no visits during Mass at 11am & 7.30pm), Sun Mass 10am, 1pm & 7.30pm

Interpretation Centre for the Jewish Quarter of Seville (Centro de Interpretación Judería de Sevilla) (Santa Cruz), Calle Ximénez de Enciso 22, normally daily 11am–7pm

Juan Foronda (Santa Cruz), Calle Sierpes 33, Mon–Fri 9.45am–8.30pm, Sat 10.15am–8.30pm

Mercado de Feria (La Macarena), Calle Feria, Mon–Sat 8am–12am

Metropol Parasol (La Macarena), Plaza de la Encarnación, observation decks and skywalks daily 9.30am–12.30am

Museo Bellver (Santa Cruz), Calle Fabiola 5, Tue – Sun 11am–8pm

Museum of Fine Arts (Museo de Bellas Artes) (El Arenal), Plaza del Museo 9, Aug Tue–Sun 9am–3pm, Sep–Jul Tue–Sat 9am–9pm, Sun 9am–3pm

Museum of the Castle of San Jorge (Museo Del Castillo De San Jorge) (Triana), Plaza del Altozano, currently closed for restoration

Museum of Popular Arts and Customs (Museo de Artes y Costumbres Populares) (Parque de María Luisa), Mudéjar Pavilion (Pabellón Mudéjar), Plaza de América 3, Tue–Sun 9am–3pm

Palacio de las Dueñas (La Macarena), Calle Dueñas 5, daily 10am–5.15pm

Parliament of Andalucia (Parlamento de Andalucía), La Macarena, Calle San Juan de Ribera, guided visits only mid-Sep to mid-Jun by appointment only tel. 954-59-59-29 or www.parlamentode andalucia.es; passports must be shown on entry

Plaza de Armas Shopping Centre (Centro Comercial Plaza de Armas) (El Arenal), Plaza la Légion, daily 9am–1am

Plaza de Toros de la Maestranza (El Arenal), Paseo de Cristóbal Colón 12, guided tours Apr–Oct 9.30am–9pm, Nov–Mar 9.30am–7pm (9.30am–3pm on bullfight days, which are staged intermittently on Sun evenings between Easter and Oct)

Real Alcázar de Sevilla (Santa Cruz), Plaza del Triunfo, Oct–Mar daily 9.30am–5pm, Apr–Sep 9.30am–7pm; night-time guided tours Mar & Oct 7.30, 8, 8.30 & 9pm, Apr–Sep 9.30, 10 & 10.30pm

Royal Shipyard of Seville (Reales Atarazanas de Sevilla), El Arenal, Calle Temprado, opening 2024

Royal Tobacco Factory (Real Fábrica de Tabacos), Parque de María Luisa, Calle San Fernando, Mon–Thu 8am–9pm, Sat 8am–7pm

Seville Aquarium (Acuario de Sevilla) (Parque de María Luisa), Muelle de las Delicias, Sep–Jun Mon–Fri 10am–8pm, Sat & Sun 10am–7pm, Jul & Aug Mon–Fri 10am–6pm, Sat & Sun 10am–8pm

Seville Cathedral (Catedral de Sevilla) (Santa Cruz), Avenida de la Constitución, Mon–Sat 10.45am–5pm, Sun 2.30–6pm; rooftop tours visit www.catedralde sevilla.es

Torre del Oro (El Arenal), Paseo de Cristóbal Colón, Mon–Fri 9.30am–6.45pm, Sat & Sun 10.30am–6.45pm

The Torre de Perdigones (Shot Tower) on Calle Resolana (see no. 95)

Bibliography

GUIDEBOOKS

The Ultimate Local's Guide to Seville (José M. Bejarano Cabrera), Independent, 2020

Secret Seville (Ricardo de Castro), Jonglez, 2022

Catedral de Sevilla (Carlos Giordano Rodríguez & Nicolás Palmisano Sosa), Edición Visuel – Serie Arquitectura, dosde, 2018

Real Alcázar de Sevilla (Carlos Giordano Rodríguez & Nicolás Palmisano Sosa), Edición Visuel – Serie Arquitectura, dosde, 2018

The Rough Guide to Andalucia (Eva Hibbs), Rough Guides, 2018

Andaluciá (Michael Jacobs), Pallas Athene, 2014

The Companion Guide to the South of Spain (Alfonso Lowe), Boydell & Brewer, 2000

Lonely Planet Andalucía (Isabella Noble et al), Lonely Planet, 2019

Eyewitness Travel Guide Seville & Andalucía (Various), Dorling Kindersley, 2020

Seville Everyman MapGuide (Various), Everyman Guides, 2018

ART AND ARCHITECTURE

Andalusian Tilework: The Art of Ceramic Decoration (Carlos Giordano Rodríguez & Nicolás Palmisano Sosa), dosde, 2018

The Cathedral of Seville (Luis Martinez Montile & Alfredo J. Morales), Scala Publishers Ltd., 1999

The Royal Palace of Seville (Alfredo J. Morales & Juan Carlos Hernandez Nunez), Scala Publishers Ltd., 1999

What Is a Bridge? The Making of Calatrava's Bridge in Seville (Spiro N. Pollalis), MIT Press Cambridge, 1999

Houses and Palaces of Andalusia (Francesco Venturi & Patricia Espinosa De Los Monteros), Scriptum, 2002

Art and Ritual in Golden-Age Spain (Susan Verdi Webster), Princeton University Press, 1998

HISTORY

The Spanish Civil War (Antony Beevor), Orbis Publishing, 2002

The Spanish Labyrinth (Gerald Brenan), Cambridge University Press, 2015

Modern Spain (1875–1980) (Raymond Carr), Oxford University Press, 2001

Spain: A History (Raymond Carr), Oxford University Press, 2001

Velazquez in Spain (David Davies), Yale University Press, 1996

The Arts of Intimacy: Christians, Jews and Muslims in the Making of Castilian Culture (Jerrilynn Dodds), Yale University Press, 2009

Moorish Spain (Richard Fletcher), Weidenfeld & Nicolson, 2001

White Wall of Spain: The Mysteries of Andalusian Culture (Allen Josephs), Iowa State Press, 1983

Contemporary Spain: A Handbook (Christopher J. Ross et al), Routledge, 2016

Andalus: Unlocking the Secrets of Moorish Spain (Jason Webster), Black Swan, 2013

The Story of Spain (Mark Williams), Santana Books, 2010

ILLUSTRATED BOOKS

Seville: A City of Art and Traditions (Daniel R. Caruncho & Ignacio Gonzáles), dosde, 2018

BULLFIGHTING AND FLAMENCO

Bulls, Bullfighting and Spanish Identities (Carrie B. Douglass), University of Arizona Press, 1999

Death in the Afternoon (Ernest Hemingway), Arrow, 1994

The Dangerous Summer (Ernest Hemingway), Simon & Schuster, 1997

In Search of Duende (Federico Garcia Lorca), New Directions, 2010

Bullfighting: Art, Technique and Spanish Society (John McCormick, Transaction Publishers, 1997),

Duende: A Journey in Search of Flamenco (Jason Webster), Black Swan, 2004

FOOD AND DRINK

Foods and Wines of Spain (Penelope Casas), Alfred A. Knopf, 1991

Tapas: The Little Dishes of Spain (Penelope Casas), Alfred A. Knopf, 2007

Andaluz: A Food Journey through Southern Spain (Fiona Dunlop), Interlink Books, 2019

The Wines of Spain (Julian Jeffs), Mitchell Beazley, 2006

Andalusia: Recipes from Seville and Beyond (Jose Pizarro), Hardie Grant, 2019

FICTION, POETRY AND TRAVEL WRITING

South from Granada: A Sojourn in Southern Spain (Gerald Brenan), Penguin Classics, 2008

Andalucia: A Literary Guide for Travellers (Andrew and Suzanne Edwards). I. B. Tauris, 2016

Poems of Arab Andalusia (Cola Franzen), City Lights Publishers, 1990

A Tomb in Seville (Norman Lewis), Eland Publishing Ltd., 2014

Travellers' Tales Spain: True Stories (Ed. Lucy McCauley), Traveller's Tales Incorporated, 2002

Iberia (James Michener), Dial Press, 2015

Miracle in Seville (James Michener), Dial Press, 2014

The Seville Communion (Arturo Peréz-Reverte), Vintage, 1997

TOUR COMPANIES

www.sevilletoursco.com
www.sevillawalkingtours.com

WEBSITES

www.exploreseville.com
www.vistsevilla.es
www.inyourpocket.com/seville
www.curiosasevilla.blogspot.com
www.andalucia.com

Acknowledgements

For kind permission to take photographs, as well as for arranging access and the provision of information, the following people are most gratefully acknowledged:

Bar El Comercio, Fabiola Cacin (Centro Andaluz de Arte Contemporáneo), Juan Carlos Mateos López & Tina Panadero (Museo del Baile Flamenco), Casa Moreno, El Rinconcillo, Nicky Gardner (Hidden Europe), Joaquin Gonzalez (Iglesia de San Luis de los Franceses), Cervecería Giralda, Jane & Emily Hale, Daniel Kennedy, Alejandro Medwedyk, Juan Monje (Corralón de Pelicano), Christian Muhr, Museo de Bellas Artes, Dave Part, Marek Pryjomko, Victoria Requeni (Corral del Conde), Jaz Rezkane, Fiona Richards, Adrian Smith, Sister Bernarda and Cristina Diaz (Convento de Santa Paula), Manolo Tiziano (Antigüedad El Pianillo), Alejandro Varela and Nicole, and John Waller.

Special thanks go to Ekke Wolf (www.typic.at) for creating the layout, Simon Laffoley for reworking several of my photos, Carolina Pacheco for the comfortable accommodation, my mother Mary and great cousin James Dickinson for bringing interesting news items to my attention, and to Digital Bits for managing my websites.

Special thanks to Roswitha Reisinger for her tireless support of my work and great company on field trips, and my late father Trevor for inspiring me to track down things unique, hidden and unusual in the first place.

Imprint

2nd Edition published by The Urban Explorer, 2023
A division of Duncan J. D. Smith
contact@duncanjdsmith.com
www.onlyinguides.com
www.duncanjdsmith.com

Graphic design: Stefan Fuhrer
Typesetting, picture editing and cover design: Ekke Wolf (www.typic.at)
Maps: www.scalablemaps.com
Printed and bound in Dubai by Oriental Press

MIX
Paper | Supporting
responsible forestry
FSC® C004800